LIVING RESPONSIVELY

THEOLOGICAL REFLECTIONS
on
LIVING in RELATIONSHIPS

Marvin P. Hoogland

with editing by Thelma Hoogland

LUCAS
PARK
BOOKS

ST. LOUIS, MISSOURI

Works Cited

Holy Bible, Revised Standard Version, multiple references.

Holy Bible, New International Version, single reference (Genesis 3:6).

Calvin, John. "Commentary on John 13." "Calvin's Commentary on the Bible." "http://studylight.org/commentaries/cal/view.cgi?bk=42&ch=13."

Berkhof, Louis, *Systematic Theology.* books.biblical training.org/Systematic Theology by Louis Berkhof.pdf, p. 85 ("The Sovereign Will of God," part d. "God's will in relation to sin").

The Heidelberg Catechism. heidelberg-catechism.com/pdf/lords-days/Heidelberg-Catechism.PDF, p. 1, pp.7-18.

Print ISBN: 9781603500616

Published by Lucas Park books
www.lucasparkbooks.com

Printed in the United States of America

TABLE of CONTENTS

Part II: RESPONSIVE LIVING in a REDEEMED WORLD

FOREWORD

As he progressed through his college years and beyond, my husband became more and more the dedicated theologian. During our years in Amsterdam, where he studied at the Free University under Professor G.C. Berkouwer and earned his doctoral degree, I was privileged to be the proverbial "fly on the wall" during many of his lively theological discussions with other university students. Already as a first year seminarian he had riled the conservative church leaders of his denomination by daring to question, in print, the proper use of the term "infallibility" in relation to Scripture.

During his years as a pastor he again earned the ire of the conservatives in the denomination by daring to defend, also in writing, the theology of one of his former professors who was being charged with seeking to undermine Christian faith; Marvin believed that this teacher was simply "addressing the various questions which arise out of the particular age in which he lives."

A career change to fulltime pastoral counseling freed him from such intense scrutiny of his theology, but did not diminish his interest in theological questions. As he notes in the introduction to this book, "old theological issues....took on new meanings in the light of [the] painful human experience" encountered in the lives of his counselees. This book is the result of his efforts to tease out how the two–theology and human need–interact.

Much of this writing was done during his retirement years. At the time of his death, which occurred within less than three weeks of our having enjoyed a 15-mile bike ride with our family, this work remained unpublished. Because death had claimed him unexpectedly, it took quite some time for me to adjust to this new stage of my life, but eventually I found time and energy to give his writing a thorough reading, and I decided that there was too much of value in this manuscript for it to remain unpublished. There were some issues of sentence structure and punctuation that needed to be addressed, some ideas needed to be expressed a bit more clearly, and a few small portions simply needed to be cut out, but the whole is essentially Marvin's writing, and in it his voice can be heard loud and clear. His "Introduction" will acquaint you with him as a person; the first half of the book will acquaint you with him as a theologian; the second half will acquaint you with him as a pastoral counselor. I am confident that you will enjoy getting to know him.

Thelma Hoogland

INTRODUCTION

Theology, often considered an esoteric intellectual exercise, is actually a very human endeavor. But can it be called fun? Or is it too serious for that? Can it be both serious and fun? Is it an academic discipline, or an enjoyable diversion? The science of things divine, or an artistic creation?

Thirty-five years ago I was taught in seminary classes that theology is indeed a science. I bought that, then. Now, I am not so sure. Really good science involves creative imagination, just as do the arts. And really good art may produce fresh insight into the nature of reality more profound than anything discovered in the sciences.

Theology itself can be pursued in a variety of ways. Influenced by the personality and life history of the writer, or by the temper of the times, it may be more like or less like either science or art. Eighteenth-century Christian theologians–Roman Catholic, Lutheran, and Reformed alike–all wrote theology in the form of a rationally coherent system that defined and refined truths of Scripture (and tradition) down to the finest detail. Theology gave the impression that it offered near-scientific proof and certainty. Theological writings then, as now, reflected the age in which they were written. Even the classic creeds of the three above-named traditions reflect the emerging suppositions of that rationalism.

Today, however, few theologians still write theology in that scholastic mold. Theology today is more likely to be written in the service of some other passion. It may be written in the context of world poverty and hunger and the social injustice that underlies these human conditions; it may be written to address theologically other issues of our living in a broken world–global issues of human rights or of environmental concern, social issues of human gender roles or of racial equality, or individual issues of commitment and broken relationships, of shame and forgiveness. Instead of trying to emulate the empirical sciences, theology today is more likely to resemble sociology or popular psychology or self-help thinking.

Who is to say how theology should be written? We may be the richer today because of the variety of ways in which theological reflections are expressed. But because theology is a human endeavor, every attempt to theologize will contain limitations and distortions. On the one hand, theology suffers whenever it pretends to be a purely objective account of God, of Scripture, or of moral truths. On the other hand, theology also suffers when it claims to be no more than one person's subjective musings on the meaning of life. The first is a form of idolatry and, as such, limits our vision of God; it is serious without being much fun. The second reduces theology to mere relativism; it may be fun, but is largely irrelevant.

Theology cannot arise or thrive in a vacuum. Christian theology has three specific reference points. The first is the Christian Scriptures, comprised of the Old Testament and the New Testament; the second lies in the history of Christian thought and practice—the traditions of the church; and the third is the theologian's contemporary milieu. Each of these three reference points plays a significant and inescapable role in doing theology. A rich diversity is added to the theological landscape by the varied ways in which theologians draw on each reference point and relate each to the others; when any one of these perspectives is ignored or minimized the theological landscape is impoverished.

The first reference point—the Scriptures confessed to be the Word of God—makes it possible to take theology with utmost seriousness. The second—history and tradition—enables us to rise above the narrowness of our limited individual vision and to avoid madly scrambling after the latest cultural fads. The third—the world of our experience—makes it possible for theologizing to be fun, to be a creative activity, and perhaps even autobiographical.

I came to see my theology as an echo of my own life's journey only after I had completed this writing. The three reference points noted above now serve for me as markings along that journey's way. Early on I was raised with the conviction that the Scriptures alone are the source of our faith and theology. Then I began to realize that church tradition exercises powerful control over how we read the Scriptures. And now I have become aware that my experience in working with people as a therapist has reshaped my theological thinking.

I grew up in the parsonage, the fourth child in a family steeped in the fairly strict and legalistic traditions of Dutch Calvinism. The one thing my preacher father impressed on his children early on was the importance of our being right in our interpretation of Scripture. We Calvinists knew that we were right in our doctrinal interpretations of the Bible. That meant the Roman Catholics were wrong—in just about everything. So were the Dispensationalists, at least on the matter of Jesus' second coming. The Baptists were wrong on infant baptism. And of course the Jehovah's Witnesses were all wrong—especially the JW's! (Dad delighted in inviting the Witnesses into our living room and bombarding them with Scriptural proof that they were wrong and we were right. They usually left quite overwhelmed, even if not convinced.) Rivaling the RC's and the JW's in being wrong, of course, were the Liberals or Modernists.

As a high school sophomore doing after-hours cleaning every Saturday night at Ditmar's IGA in Galewood, Michigan, I waged incessant battle with the Baptist seminarian working with us. Dad's commentaries provided ample ammunition in my effort to prove to him from the Bible that infants had to be baptized.

Years later, as a graduate student at Indiana University, I carried on the same warfare with two Baptist seminary graduates. They were as eager combatants as I, but there is only so much one can say on the subject of infant baptism, and the discussions wore thin after a few weeks of repetitious argumentation. I clearly recall standing in their dormitory room one evening as they started in on me—as I had often enough on them. I recall a sinking feeling of futility. And then came a bright idea. Why not, I suggested, let me argue the Baptist position, and you fellows the Reformed view? Then we could learn from each other where we misunderstood. They both responded with a simple no. When pressed, they admitted, "We wouldn't know were to begin." "What!" I exclaimed, "you mean we've been arguing all these weeks and you haven't even tried to understand my point of view?" Since then I've come to realize that most theological arguments that are intent on proving oneself right and others wrong are of this kind: no one is listening to what the other side is saying. And it does not matter whether you are Baptist, Reformed, or something else.

In studying philosophy at Indiana for that one year I was introduced to the philosophy of science by Professor Norwood Hansen (killed a few years later in an airplane crash). I have always felt indebted to him. He tried in two courses to teach us something about Ludwig Wittgenstein. Wittgenstein's *Tractatus* remained a mystery to me, but from his *Philosophical Investigations* I learned to appreciate the value of looking at how words function in a specific context. I recall something about words having a "family of meanings," not just one essential meaning. I have made use of that insight in Chapter 1, examining and rejecting the word *responsibility* as a suitable companion to the term *divine sovereignty*.

While attending Calvin Seminary the following year I wrote for the student paper an article examining the word *infallibility*. I raised questions about whether the word was a suitable one for what we confessed concerning the Scriptures. Many conservatives in the church, ignoring what I had actually written, decried the supposed liberalism in the seminary that allowed such perceived attacks on the sacred Scriptures to be published. I endured hours of interrogation before I was given licensure to preach in my denomination. My older brother, also a seminarian, was initially denied candidacy for the ministry by our Synod because he had supported this "heresy" in his own writings. In the middle of that Synodical flare-up, I was married in Edgerton, Minnesota, with brother John as best man. After the wedding John, returning to stand before the Synod for further questioning, was eventually accepted as a candidate. Theology, when taken seriously, has a way of intruding on our personal lives in ways we never quite anticipate or wholly forget.

For me, however, the questions deepened. Is there something deceptive about the way we believe that our interpretations of Scripture are right? Is there something wrong with the way we insist that we alone are right?

Three years of seminary resolved few of my questions. I went on to graduate school in Amsterdam to pursue the study of systematic theology. I found the writings of G.C. Berkouwer liberating, and the work of Karl Barth inspiring. But I also discovered in the writings of John Calvin a perspective that was both pastoral and ecumenical. Calvin's perspective on the exaltation of Christ (my dissertation topic) avoided the problems that later divided Lutherans and Calvinists of the next generation (who, sad to say, returned to the ways of scholastic rationalism). In retrospect I realize that reading Calvin stimulated my search for a theology that could be solidly biblical and at the same time ecumenical. It is my hope that this present work will contribute to that elusive goal.

But before I could seriously pursue such a goal I had to learn not to take theology quite so seriously. I had to learn to take people, as individuals functioning in the matrix of all their significant relationships, more seriously. Incessantly pursuing theology can lead one to ignore or avoid what is important in people's lives.

Serving as pastor in a small north central Iowa farming community provided a context for learning what is more important than being right. Several persons in the congregation suffered from depression. A marriage was in serious trouble. A husband experienced paranoid delusions. An unmarried teen became pregnant. Being right somehow seemed less important than being helpful. And, though I asked advice from the good folks at the nearby mental health facility, and took a week of workshops at a psychiatric hospital, I wasn't at all sure how to be helpful.

In 1969 I accepted the opportunity to become a campus pastor at the University of Illinois in Champaign-Urbana. But the transition was not smooth. Neighboring ministers back in small town Iowa churches protested some views I had expressed about a Dutch theologian whom they "knew" to be wrong—without having read his work. Subjected to a day-long interrogation and eventually suspended from the ministry for three months, I proceeded to appeal to our denominational Synod on procedural grounds. My appeal was successful, and, a year after having arrived, I was reinstated and finally installed in my new position. My confidence that the church really is concerned with the truth of Scripture and the gospel, however, was not fully restored.

That year the U. of I. campus exploded with student strikes, demonstrations, and the "trashing" of local business places in the name of justice and in opposition to an unjust war. The National Guard was out in force. With my ministry efforts geared toward students and addressing their needs, I became a trained selective service counselor; I also joined other clergy in being available to counsel pregnant young women who were considering abortion. For a year I attended weekly sessions for clergy at the local mental health center to gain some awareness of differing counseling perspectives. I saw my ministry in those years as a ministry of presence, modeled after God's presence with us in the incarnation.

Meanwhile, the board under which I worked had become enamored with the church growth movement. This I increasingly saw as the church's selling its soul for a popular model derived from

big business, much like the church in the early Middle Ages sold out
to the state by modeling itself after the Roman Empire. Through
all of this my disillusionment with the church and its theology was
growing. I saw little genuine interest in or reward for searching the
Scriptures for new understandings to grapple with new times. I
became convinced that "doing theology" was a futile task without
a supportive community.

After five years in a rewarding ministry to students I sought out
formal training in doing therapy, something that appeared to offer
a far more promising way of helping people than doing theology.
Since 1975 I have been doing just that–doing therapy instead of
doing theology. Except that, along the way, a funny thing happened.
The more I was with people in their struggles and in their pain,
the more I found myself reflecting anew on the meaning of the
gospel and the message of the Scriptures. I began to realize that
an obsession with being right, and proving others wrong, is not
limited to theologians and ministers. In fact, it invades nearly every
marriage whenever conflict emerges. Could that obsession be close
to the core issue in all sin?

Thus, old theological issues refused to go away. They took on
new meanings in the light of painful human experience. Trying to
help people work through the brokenness of their relationships,
I found it helpful to draw on religious meanings. And I began to
wonder–which has the greater influence on the other: theology
on the lives of people, or meeting people in their struggles on an
understanding of theology? Having been trained in the "family
systems" approach to therapy, I came to appreciate the value of
seeing each as influencing and enriching the other in circular
fashion.

It is my hope that working as a therapist has indeed deepened
my theological understandings in a way that may also be helpful
to others, no matter what their theological tradition may be. It has
actually been fun for me to uncover connections between a renewed
theological perspective and the significant relationships of life.

These connections are brought to light in both parts of this
work. Part I explores some basic theological principles that lie at
the root of all human relationships. Part II weaves those principles
in and through the various relationships that impact our lives–as

individuals, in marriage, in parenting, in the church as the body of Christ, and as Christians living in God's broken but redeemed world.

At the same time, these theological reflections seek to find a place within the history of Christian thought and tradition. Chapter I sheds light on the age-old tension between divine sovereignty and human responsibility and freedom. The central thesis of this work is that God created us to be responsive; *responsivity* best expresses our relationship to God. *Responsibility*, on the other hand, is a concept that originates with the fall and reflects the brokenness of human life, and is therefore unsuited to be in correlation with divine sovereignty. The course of human responsivity is followed through the traditional schema of creation, fall, and redemption, and then applied to living responsively in all of life's relationships.

One's beginning point of reference may be the most important of all. My concern throughout has been to give expression to the message of grace that permeates the Christian Scriptures. Only as a theology faithfully reflects that message is it worthy of being taken seriously.

My wish is that you, dear reader, may have as much enjoyment in perusing these theological reflections as I have had in formulating them.

LIVING
RESPONSIVELY

Part I

THEOLOGICAL PERSPCECTIVES
on
DIVINE SOVEREIGNTY
and
HUMAN RESPONSIVITY

1

SOVEREIGNTY AND RESPONSIBILITY:

A Correlation in Need of Correction

Sovereignty: "Supreme excellence...supreme power... free from external control." (*Merriam-Webster's Collegiate Dictionary*. 10th Ed. 1998. Print)

Responsibility: "Moral, legal, or mental accountability... something for which one is responsible." (Ibid.)

Divine sovereignty: "God chose you from the beginning to be saved" (II Thessalonians 2:13). "This is not your own doing, it is the gift of God" (Ephesians 2:8).

Human responsibility: "Your faith has saved you; go in peace" (Luke 7:50). "Work out your own salvation with fear and trembling" (Philippians 2:12).

Throughout the history of the church the attempt to hold fast to both the sovereignty of God and the responsibility of human beings has produced a continuing struggle. In that struggle, no one denies that sovereignty belongs to God or that responsibility belongs to man. But, we ask, in what way does God's sovereignty come to expression if human responsibility is to be considered significant? Conversely, in what way is there room for responsibility genuinely to function in light of God's mighty sovereignty?

Theologians, preachers, and even ordinary believers have wrestled through the centuries with the problem of how to relate these two articles of faith to each other. The dominant tendency in the history of the church has been to begin by assuming the importance of human responsibility, and then to adjust the idea of divine sovereignty to it. If faith is essential to salvation, and freedom is essential to human dignity, then any understanding of divine sovereignty that compromises the response of faith as being our own cannot be tolerated. Some describe God's sovereignty as an omniscient eternal foreknowledge of those who will believe and will thus belong to the elect; God is seen as offering the gift of his saving grace to us, but in the end it will be our own responsibility to receive and accept that gift. However, the uneasy question still remains: Does our act of faith in this way limit the sovereignty of God?

A less common tendency goes in the opposite direction. We can begin by assuming the full reality of God's sovereignty, and then proceed to adapt the idea of human responsibility to that. In this view God in his sovereignty not only foreknows, but also decrees, who will be saved and who will be lost; history is then the outworking of those decrees as God's Spirit works conversion and faith in those whom God has decreed to save, and the others God leaves to their own destruction. Some theologians have implied that sovereignty excludes God's granting any grace at all, even a well-meant offer of salvation, to those who disbelieve, and yet their unbelief is still said to be their own; they are responsible for their own rejection of the gospel, and for their eternal damnation.

It appears, then, that we can either have a belief in human responsibility that leaves us with a compromised version of God's sovereignty, or we can have a confession of God's sovereignty that leaves us unconvinced that our own response of belief or unbelief really makes any difference at all.

Mainline Reformed thought has characteristically attempted to boldly assert both the sovereignty of God and the full responsibility of human beings, without any real effort to reconcile the two. Let them both stand side by side, we are told. Let them be in tension. If they seem to contradict each other, hold on to both as equally reflecting the truth taught in the Scriptures. Let the apparent contradictions be a confession of our human limitation, an acknowledgement that God's ways are higher than our ways, an expression of humility before the face of God.

There might, however, be a better way. What if we were to stand back and recognize that the term *responsibility* has too many meanings associated with it—most of them presupposing our brokenness—to be very helpful? Then, I believe, we could go on to have a theological discussion of God's role and our own response that is more than an exercise in theoretical semantics with limited significance for the lives that most of us live in our relationships with others, more than mere conjecture regarding the faith upon which we draw as we struggle with daily concerns.

The Many Faces of Responsibility

Allow me to elaborate. The term *responsibility* is a rich concept precisely because it includes within it a wide variety of specific meanings. At the same time, that variety of meanings can make the term a confusing one to use. Consider some of the meanings associated with this term.

Responsibility as Duty or Obligation

To say that I have a responsibility to pay my taxes means that I have a solemn duty, as an obligation of my citizenship, to do so. Or, to say that I have a responsibility to remain faithful to my wife implies that fidelity is an obligation I have taken on myself upon making my marriage vows; love, we recognize, is a commitment which carries with it obligations and duties—responsibilities.

When we talk about human responsibility as it relates to divine sovereignty, we express an awareness that God's sovereign control of all things does not exclude our having duties and obligations, most of which are summarized in the biblical Ten Commandments.

Responsibility as Blame or Guilt

If I find a lamp lying broken on the floor, I may well exclaim, "Who's responsible for this?" I am not then talking about anyone's duty or obligation. I am asking, rather, who is to blame, who is the guilty party? The teacher who finds that there is money missing from her desk drawer may inform the class that they are all to stay in the classroom until the responsible party comes forward. She needs to find who is guilty. To be responsible is to be blameworthy, to be guilty.

To assert human responsibility in the face of divine sovereignty is to affirm that God's sovereignty over all things does not remove us from blame or guilt. God's sovereign providence may be at work in all that we do, but we are nonetheless held to be guilty, blameworthy, for our own sinful actions.

Responsibility as Acceptance of Consequences

When we teach our children that they must learn to take responsibility for their own behavior, we are teaching them more than the importance of acknowledging guilt. We are also teaching them that their actions carry with them certain consequences that they must accept. Actions have natural consequences. If you stay up all night partying before an exam, you will not likely function well in writing the exam; you may fail. Likewise, if I drive over the speed limit I may be setting myself up for being fined, or, worse, for causing a serious accident; when I am guilty of breaking the law I will need to accept the consequences of actions for which I am responsible.

Thus when we pair human responsibility with divine sovereignty we express an awareness that not just our actions, but the consequences of our actions, including the eternal consequences of our unbelief, may rightly be attributed to our own doing.

Responsibility as Accountability

This meaning seems to be the literal one suggested in the Dutch word *verantwoordelijkheid* (or German *verantwortlichkeit*) which could be translated "answerableness." To say that we have responsibility often means that we can be held accountable for what we do. We have to answer for our actions. When I accept responsibility for managing a project I may be talking about more than a duty which I accept, more than my willingness to accept blame for possible mistakes, and more than acceptance of the consequences that follow its failure or success. I am saying that I am accepting the fact that others have the right to question me about how I have managed the project, and that I am ready to answer for or give public account of what I have done. I am accountable.

This sense of our accountability is implied when we talk about human responsibility in relation to divine sovereignty. We are saying that we are legitimately held accountable for what we do. We will answer for our behavior. A day of judgment, a time of accountability, is coming.

Responsibility as Freedom for Moral Choice

Still another meaning of the concept of responsibility is that we have the capacity for, and freedom of, choice. We can choose between alternatives. We can choose between right and wrong. Much of our job in parenting our children involves teaching them the difference between right and wrong as we seek to strengthen their desire and ability to choose what is right and good.

When we affirm human responsibility, we are asserting that our actions really are freely of our own doing and our own moral choosing. We are not robots, but are free and responsible human beings.

Responsibility as Maturity

Another dimension of responsibility, as we commonly use the term, refers to a coming to maturity. The immature child has not yet developed a sense of responsibility. An adolescent boy who neglects his homework, stays out beyond his curfew, frequents parties where he becomes inebriated, is not acting responsibly. He is acting immaturely. (Adults, though they are expected to display responsibility, will at times also act immaturely—that is, not responsibly.)

When we have maturity in mind as the meaning of responsibility, we will probably be implying all the earlier-noted meanings as these have developed in a person's progression from the immaturity of childhood to the maturity of adulthood: maturity involves the readiness to accept obligations, to acknowledge one's own guilt, to accept consequences, and to be held accountable; maturity also involves exercising one's capacity to choose what is good and right rather than playing the helpless child or victim role. Responsibility is a mark of maturity.

Christian thought affirms the significance of all of these dimensions of responsibility. It affirms, at the same time, the reality of divine sovereignty. What Christian thought has nearly always rejected is the notion of determinism. If talk of election and predestination, of divine providence, and of salvation "by grace alone" seem logically to imply a form of determinism, such an implication of human logic has simply been rejected. Where divine sovereignty is held without compromise, as in some forms of Calvinism, the tension between the two is simply accepted with an appeal to the mystery of God's infinite and eternal ways, along with the need for humility on our part.

The Question of Free Will

The same tension is evident in the philosophical and theological questions of human responsibility–free will. Here, however, the issue becomes more focused. We have no difficulty ascribing free will to human beings when referring to the various dimensions of responsibility identified above. But when the question focuses on our capacity to earn salvation and achieve union with God on our own (or with partial help from God), Augustinian Christianity has denied that we have a free will that enables us to achieve this blessedness.

Some (including John Calvin) maintain that though we were created with free will, this freedom was lost by the fall into sin. Before the fall we were *posse non pecare*, able not to sin–that was our freedom. After the fall we became *non posse non pecare*, not able not to sin–our freedom, our free will, was lost. Now, though we are born into a fallen world, bearers of the original sin that infects our whole being, responsibility in all the various meanings we have noted is still ours. Accepting such responsibility, however, is not sufficient to reunite us in blessedness with God. No amount of fulfilling of duty, admission of blame, acceptance of consequences, holding oneself accountable, making moral choices, or growing in maturity will be sufficient to return us to God. In that regard we are helpless, "dead through our trespasses" (Ephesians 2:5), bereft of our free will.

And thus the paradox, bringing us right back to where we started. If we truly believe that sovereignty belongs to God, the author of life and salvation, who freely bestows love and grace on those whom he chooses, then that belief brings us to a point where human responsibility is of no account. On the other hand, however much we affirm responsibility in most areas of human life, in the final and most important arena of all, the arena of faith and eternal destiny, human responsibility appears to fail us. And so we face a choice. We can either hold to divine sovereignty by acknowledging the limitations of human responsibility and freedom, or we can modify and limit divine sovereignty by making our act of faith–rather than God's grace alone–the crucial and decisive factor in salvation. Pelagianism, Roman Catholicism, Arminianism, liberalism, and American fundamentalism have all done the latter in significant ways.

A third option, that of grasping the dilemma by both its horns and clinging to each, contrary to all logic and human understanding, is what Calvinists have been prone to do. We can assert human responsibility to the fullest extent, they say, while continuing to profess full confidence in God's unlimited sovereignty as we stand in awe before the mystery of God's working, maintaining humility before God while suspending human logic. In this spirit Louis Berkhof (1873-1957) writes in his *Systematic Theology*, "Problems arise here which have never yet been solved and which are probably incapable of solution by man."

In Search of a Connection

What Christian theology has often failed to note is that these problems arise when, at the outset, we separate God and humanity. We take either the concept of divine sovereignty or that of human responsibility and define each in terms of itself alone, and then go on to talk about traits of each independently of the other. If we start with God and construct an abstract definition for his sovereignty, we will be hard pressed to give any real meaning to human responsibility and free will. On the other hand, if we start by defining human responsibility as an inherent trait found in each person as an individual, we will be equally hard pressed to honor the full sovereignty of God.

Nor is the dilemma resolved when we take each concept and define its meaning separately and then let the two simply stand side by side with no inner connection. What we have failed to recognize is that *"sovereignty" and "responsibility" are both relational terms*. Is not divine sovereignty a meaningless concept applied to God-in-himself or to the Trinity by itself? Apart from creation, over what or whom is God the sovereign Lord? And what possible meaning can responsibility have if we look only at an isolated individual apart from any relationship to God or to another human being? To whom might such an isolated one be responsible?

When we begin, however, by seeing God and his human image-bearers in an intimate relationship to each other, the dilemmas fade into obscurity. Now our search leads us to identify the meaning both of divine sovereignty and of human responsibility *within the context of that relationship*, and we can see the two concepts in an inseparable correlation that preserves the integrity of each.

Seen at the outset as part of God's relationship to the human race, divine sovereignty need not be understood simply in terms of pure power and control, nor as a merely linear causality. Instead we can see that it is an integral part of God's love, caring, and grace toward his creatures. God's sovereignty, his "supreme excellence," is at work in his creating a world with creatures whom he can love and who can freely love him in return. His sovereignty calls for, and calls forth, a *response from* all his creatures.

Also at the outset, from the first days of creation, the human pair, the first man and woman, are created with the capacity to be responsive to the love and goodness of the sovereign Lord who created them. God's sovereignty inherently looks to human responsiveness for its fulfillment. Thus human responsibility takes on meaning from the very beginning as a *response to* God's own creative love and goodness and grace and purpose.

There is one further step that we need to take in our search for a connection between divine sovereignty and human responsibility: we need to recognize that part of the difficulty lies in the word *responsibility* itself. As we noted earlier, any single use of the word will refer to one or another of a variety of meanings, but never to all of them at the same time. In the statement, "I have a responsibility to remain faithful to my spouse," for instance, *duty* serves as an appropriate synonym. On the other hand, referring to the broken lamp mentioned earlier, the intended meaning of "Who's responsible for this?" is "Who is guilty?" In this case, the other meanings enumerated—duty, consequences, accountability, moral choice, maturity—do not function as synonyms. Thus, because the meaning shifts from one context to another, we find that the word *responsibility* proves to be inherently too fragmented, too broken into pieces, to be really useful for illuminating our created and redeemed relationship to a sovereign God. And too many of its meanings are darkened by a reference point located in the fall; its meaning of guilt, of the need to choose between good and evil, and even those meanings of duty and accountability, with implications of dire consequences, all carry with them a tone of foreboding that is shaped by the fall and the law rather than by creation or by redemption and grace.

We need to find some other word to correlate with divine sovereignty. Beneath the various connotations of responsibility lies another concept which is both deeper and broader, and which expresses well what it means to be a human being in relationship to God, whether by creation, in the fall, or through redemption: *To be a human being is to have the capacity to be responsive.*

The English word responsibility connotes an "ability" to "respond." This capacity, this ability to respond, we can call our *responsivity*; this capacity in action we can call our *responsiveness*. I propose, then, that instead of juxtaposing divine sovereignty with human *responsibility* we, instead, juxtapose God's sovereignty with human *responsivity,* defining each of them in relation to the other at the outset. Divine sovereignty in this sense refers to God's creative power by which he calls forth a world which he can rule with his goodness and grace, according to his own loving purpose, and bring to life creatures who respond to him with praise and adoration. Human responsivity, in turn, is that uniquely human capacity to respond to the Creator with loving obedience in recognition of God as the author of life, the fountain of love and of all things good. That responsivity will be evident in our relationships to all of creation, and it will especially come to the fore in our human relationships.

Human responsivity, as here understood, is not something that is, or even seems to be, restricted by divine sovereignty. Quite the contrary, our responsivity is potentially infinite even though we are finite. We have the capacity to be responsive to all of creation and to all other human beings; we also have the capacity to be responsive to the eternal, infinite, and all-caring Creator and Redeemer who showers us with his redemptive grace and love and peace. To whatever degree we grow in our experience and understanding of God's sovereign purpose—of his love, grace, and peace—to that extent our own responsiveness grows and expands rather than being restricted or compromised. (When I think of our essential humanness in terms of this capacity of ours to be responsive, I begin to appreciate the excitement and wonder that David expresses in Psalm 8 about the glory and dignity of man—made but a little lower than the angels, or than God himself!)

Divine sovereignty, God's creative power and loving rule, is not something that is threatened or restricted by human responsivity. The more our responsiveness comes into play in the interrelationship between ourselves and God, the more his sovereign grace and love and purpose are experienced and celebrated. Rather than being restricted, God's sovereign name is magnified!

The usual tension between divine sovereignty and human *responsibility* is resolved when we correlate God's sovereignty, instead, with human *responsivity*. There are no duties that we are obligated to fulfill which are impossible to carry out, for which we will be eternally condemned; what we cannot do is exactly what we are warned against attempting to do, namely, trying to please God apart from acknowledging him as the source of all goodness. What is impossible is to develop a saving faith on our own that ignores or denies God's grace, but no one is expected to do this impossible thing. No one will ever be held accountable or condemned for this failure. This failure is predicted in the Scriptures.

The gospel calls people everywhere back to a response of simple faith in the grace of the sovereign God. Within that relationship of renewed trust our freedom is restored, and God is again glorified. The tension is transformed into a creative relationship which is mutually enhancing to creature and to Creator alike.

So let's take a journey to explore some of the interplay between God's sovereignty and our human responsivity. We will look at the creation stories of Genesis 1 and 2 to get a sense of the responsivity that embraces sovereignty. We will look at what happens to that responsivity in the story of the fall into sin. We will inquire about the renewal of responsivity through the coming of Jesus Christ. And we will examine anew the meaning of Christian faith, hope, and love for this life and for eternity in the light of that fascinating interplay of human responsivity and divine sovereignty.

After these heady theological excursions in Part I, we will explore in Part II some of the ways in which our renewed individual responsivity comes to expression in responsive living within the important relationships of our lives—in marriage, family, church, and society.

2

IN GOD'S IMAGE:

Responsivity in Creation

The two creation stories in Genesis 1 and 2 compliment each other beautifully. The first story highlights the majestic sovereignty of God's power: as he but speaks, creation springs into being. The second creation account tells the story from the point of view of the first human pair and their response to God's provision.

The unity of the two stories is found in something other than the detailed ordering of events in the respective accounts. The sequence of events is so strikingly different in the two accounts that the very juxtaposition of the two stories informs us that "right sequence" is not a matter of concern. The unity lies, rather, in the correlation, the ongoing interaction, between divine sovereignty and human responsivity. Indeed, in the first story all of creation displays increasing responsiveness to the powerfully creative word of the sovereign God. And in the second story the creative provision of God experienced by the first human beings cannot but elicit a response of awestruck wonder, deep gratitude, and exultant praise.

The First Creation Story: Genesis 1

The initial creation is of an earth that is formless and empty, with darkness on the face of the deep waters. As the Spirit of God moves over these dark waters a pattern begins to emerge which, with some variations, goes like this: God speaks—something new appears which is then separated out from what was already there; God speaks again, and the newly created reality is given a name (and pronounced "good") as the old (that which had already existed) receives a new name and identity; then the new and the old in their separateness are brought together into a dynamic new whole. Both now receive their identity within this new relationship. In their unity each retains its own identity and enhances the other. In short, as the creation comes into being by the summons of the sovereign Creator, each divine word expands the responsive capacity both of the new and of the old in their interrelationship. Notice the pattern:

The Six Days of Creation

Day 1: As the Spirit of God moves over the face of the dark deep, God speaks, "Let there be light" (Gen. 1:3). The newly created light that appears in contrast to the existing darkness is pronounced "good;" then comes the separation: the light is separated from the darkness and given a new name, "Day." But through this separation and naming, the darkness now also receives a new identity: it is called "Night." And now Night and Day, evening and morning, form a new whole together: "one day." In response to the creative working of God's Spirit and Word, the darkness itself, through the creation of light, becomes more than it was. And the light, good in itself, receives an expanded identity by its separation from, and yet new unity with, the contrasting darkness.

Day 2: Then God's Word again addresses the waters over which the Spirit of God is moving, and God calls forth a new thing, a "firmament," an expanse which creates a separation between the existing waters below and the waters that are now placed above that firmament. And the new thing that separates the waters above from the waters below is given a name: "Heaven." The first separation of the waters is complete, a second day; but a further separation of the lower waters ("the waters which were under the firmament") continues into the third day.

Day 3: On the third day God speaks and calls the waters that are under heaven to be gathered together into one place so that something new can emerge: dry land appears. The separation takes place and the dry land is given a name: "Earth." But the very formation and naming of the dry land as "Earth" gives a new identity and name also to the waters from which it was separated out; the waters of the deep are now called "Seas." And once again the result is "good." By the formation of "Earth," the original waters of the deep, much like the once-foreboding darkness that hovered over them, take on a new identity and form a new whole in relation to the dry ground; Earth and Seas together now also form a new whole in relation to the expanse of the heavens above.

Thus the theme of creation unfolds. As the sovereign God expresses his powerful will, not only does something new emerge in response, but what already existed becomes something more than it was. The separation leads to a new whole which enhances the identity of each part as each is given a new name. The working of divine sovereignty, rather than restricting the responsiveness of the creation, enlarges its responsivity as the creative pattern unfolds with the formation of new correlations: God and creation, light and darkness, evening and morning, heaven and earth, dry land and seas.

And the process continues on that third day. The sovereign divine Word calls on the now already-formed earth to bring forth something new: *life*! In response, vegetation, plants and trees, are all brought forth out of the earth. Each in turn bears seeds that will continue to bring forth new produce and fruit after its kind. Not only is something new created, but the already formed earth itself becomes something new: fruitful. Fruit emerges, with seeds that go back into the fruitful earth to produce more new plants and fruit. Here again, a separation works to form a new wholeness that also enhances the identity of the earth that already existed. And God sees that the new whole is "good." And what already has been, evening and morning, produces yet a new, a third, completed day.

Day 4: Next, God's creative work returns to what is already in place, the firmament of the heavens. His Word now calls into being new lights for the heavens, a light to rule the Day and other lights to rule the Night, to enhance the separation of the light from the darkness. In the process, moreover, the earth itself is transformed, for where once darkness was upon the face of the deep, now these new heavenly bodies "give light upon the earth" (Gen. 1:15). The earth is not just fruitful but is now also full of light. In relationship to these new heavenly bodies the existing earth comes to know the four seasons and the counting of years. And here again the darkness and the light in their separation, the evening and the morning together, form a new whole: a day, the fourth new day.

Day 5: The pattern of God's sovereign creative working continues into the fifth day. Now the waters of the gathered seas produce something new and are themselves transformed, as was the earth on the third day. The waters bring forth all manner of living creatures that move about in the sea, and birds begin to fly across the heavens. It is not just that new creatures are formed. The waters themselves become something new, for we read that now "the waters swarm." What is more, the fish of the seas and the birds of the air are blessed so that they, too, multiply and fill the seas and the earth with moving life. The sovereign working of God's Word and will does not limit the creation's responsiveness. No, the creatures respond by reproducing; what once was empty and without form becomes shaped with purpose and filled with expanding life. By the end of the fifth day the waters are teeming with life that freely moves through them, and the air is filled with birds that fly and freely soar. And all that freedom is "good" in the sight of the sovereign God.

<u>Day 6</u>: It is so good that on the sixth day God turns again to the dry ground, the earth, which is already flooded with light and full of firmly rooted plants and trees that reproduce. But that's still not good enough, not free enough, for God. God now calls on the earth to produce creatures as free as those of the seas and those of the heavens: cattle, beasts, and all creeping things—creatures that are free to move about upon the earth. God's sovereign working in creation seems intent on producing creatures that increasingly respond with freedom. Rather than restricting freedom, his sovereign willing and working appear to progressively enhance the identity and freedom of his creatures.

But the sixth day is not yet complete, nor is the working of God's sovereign creative power finished. Now, however, the pattern changes slightly. God need not stay stuck in any rut (in his sovereign working God, above all, is free!). So God communes with himself. He now takes time to speak a word with himself before acting. The Spirit who once moved now stops to deliberate; the Word who before had spoken incisively now reflects before God brings forth the culmination of his creative will, before he forms a creature who, more than all the others, will be truly free—as God himself is free. God decides to create "adam," the human being, "in his own image" (Gen. 1:27). What kind of creature will this be? What will be this image-bearer's relationship to the Creator God? And what will God become in relationship to one so like God's own self?

The story focuses on two dimensions of this likeness to God found in the image-bearer: adam is created male and female, and adam, as male and female, is given dominion over all the other creatures.

God's Image as Male and Female

A striking interplay between the singular and the plural is evident in the creation of the human being, both in the deliberative planning and in the report of the completed creation. As God proposes to himself what he shall do, God says, "Let us make man [singular, *adam*, the generic *man*] in our image, after our likeness; and let them [plural] have dominion..." (Gen. 1:26). The same interplay occurs as this creation is accomplished: "So God created adam [singular] in his image, in the image of God he created him [singular]; male and female he created them [plural]" (Gen. 1:27). God's image-bearer, one who is like God himself, is both singular and plural at the same time. There is a profound oneness or unity in the adam-ness, the humanness, of the image-bearer. At the same time a significant otherness or two-ness is present here. Adam is one and yet male and female, two in contrast. The creation story is telling us that the most profound essence of being an image-bearer of the Creator is "being-in-relationship." To be human is to be in relationship. (We will be seeing more of this pattern in the second creation story.)

We have noted that in all the previous acts of creation what is newly created is either set in contrast to or comes out of something that was created before it. Light, which became Day, was separated out from the darkness, which became Night, yielding evening and morning, forming a new unity. The expanse of the heavens separated out the waters below from the waters above, and the dry land was then separated out from the waters below. Out of the land came plants and trees; out of the waters came fish (and birds?); and again, out of the earth animals emerged. In each case the new creation enhanced the identity of the old out of which it had come and with which it formed a new unity or whole.

The same implication is present in the creation of the human beings. Their essence is a reflection or image of what God is. As we consider "What is man?" we gain a clearer sense of who God is. And the greater sense we gain of who God is, the more we can understand who we are as human beings. In this creation story the human being is not said to come out of, or to be produced by, the earth or the waters. He/she emerges, instead, from out of the reflective deliberations of God within himself.

The deepest mystery of the godhead comes to expression here. God is profoundly one God, yet within that one godhead are the Father, the Word or Son, and the Spirit. From out of communing within God's self comes this new creation who is different from God and therefore set quite apart from him. And yet, as God's image, the human pair is made in God's likeness and forms a new kind of union with the Creator—a union that will enhance the identity of God, out of whom the image came, and will give to God, in turn, new names that magnify his glory. At the same time that union will enhance and expand the identity and the responsiveness of this creature who bears God's own image. The God who is truly free in his sovereignty creates in his own image a being who is also free. The more God works his will in the newly created image-bearer of himself, the more free the human pair will be. And the more this freedom comes to expression in them, the more God's name and glory will be magnified. Neither limits the other. The working of God's sovereign will and the responsiveness of God's image-bearer form a correlation, a new whole, which enhances the identity of each in relation to the other.

Although all other living creatures—plants, fish, birds, and beasts—were also given the command to be fruitful and multiply and fill the earth and the seas with life, only of the human being is it said that they are "male and female." We know that nearly all life has sexual differentiation, yet something special is indicated here about adam as male and female. We are dealing here not just with a biological reproductive capacity shared with all living creatures, but with a unique capacity for relationships that is rooted in the very ground of our being, the triune God. Already we sense that human freedom will flourish within, and only within, the context of relationships that are formed with God himself and with others who also bear his image.

In Part II we will reflect on marriage and on the family, and beyond that on human relationships within the church and within society. We will find that the mystery of the Trinity is at the heart of all growth-producing relationships, and its violation is at the root of all human problems that arise in those relationships. For now it is enough to have a hint from the creation story as to where our freedom lies: it lies in our relationship with another. This is where we will be most truly human and most truly free. We experience freedom as we discover our essential oneness with the other even while we value and benefit from the contrasting differences from the other. We live in union with the God in whose image we are made. In relation to other human beings and in relation to God, we experience an unending capacity to grow.

God's Image as Having Dominion

Sovereign dominion belongs to the triune God in all three divine persons. Similarly, in the Genesis story the dominion given to adam belongs to male and female together: "Let *them* have dominion" (1:26). Here, it seems, God is musing over the possibility of fashioning a creature made in God's own image. Letting them have dominion is not so much a mandate as it is the conceiving of a possibility in God's mind. It is as if God is letting us in on his own "thought process" as he plans our creation: if we're going to truly make a creature in our own image, let's make them one and many at the same time; what's more, let's give to them the real potential of sharing in our own free sovereignty, our dominion. And so, in verse 28, we hear God's instructions to his image-bearers: "have dominion over...every living thing."

Then, upon creating this male and female adam, God blesses them. "Be fruitful and multiply," he says—keep on creating! "Fill the earth and subdue it" (Gen. 1:29). Just as the Creator had "subdued" the deep waters of the earth that were covered with darkness, the creature is enjoined to keep on making something new out of what already exists as he/they practice the dominion given to them over the fish of the sea, the birds of the air, and the beasts of the field. And, to make the blessing complete, the Creator promises sustenance to this new creature, his image-bearer: "Behold, I have given you every plant yielding seed which is upon the face of all the earth, and every tree with seed in its fruit; you shall have them for food" (Gen. 1:29). Thus the creature's being and freedom continue to be enhanced even as the creature's dependence on God is recognized and valued.

As with each new step of creation the identity of what already existed is enhanced by its relationship to the new that is brought forth, and by the whole that the old and the new now form, note that with each step God's own identity is also enhanced. God himself also becomes more than he was. As the creation comes into being, the eternal God becomes the Creator, someone he was not apart from the creation. As light appears, he becomes the Source of Light. As life comes forth from the seas and the earth, God becomes the Author of Life. As something new is created and named, the eternal and infinite God receives a new name and a new identity. Not only does his creative and sovereign Word work continually to enhance all of creation with each act, but the creatures who appear also in turn magnify his name. As the heavens declare God's glory, God becomes one who is worthy of such glory.

And then, in forming a creature in his own image who, given dominion over all the earth, has the capacity to respond in love—as God loves—to all of creation, to one another as male and female, and to God himself, God's own identity is enlarged. God becomes more than a Creator; he becomes a Lover, a Covenant-maker. Now God's sovereignty and human responsivity, far from limiting each other, mutually enhance each other. They form a correlation, a new whole.

This newly created relationship is, indeed, full of mystery, but it is not the mystery of an intellectual puzzle. It is, instead, a mystery full of wonder at the gracious being and work of God, who is the never-ending source of goodness, life, freedom, and newness. We experience here a mystery that evokes not puzzlement, but praise and adoration in a relationship of mutual trust and love.

And so, as the creation story concludes, God rests on the seventh day. God is the Creator who praises his creation as "very good," and is in turn glorified by all of creation. God is a Lover who enjoys and is enjoyed by his Beloved.

The Second Creation Story: Genesis 2

The differences between the two creation narratives are striking. Whereas the Creator is named simply "God" in the first, he is called "the Lord God" throughout the second narrative. Whereas the first story unfolds with the seven days of creation, the second account speaks of everything as occurring within one day; the events described all take place "in the day that the Lord God made the earth and the heavens" (Gen. 2:4). Whereas in the first story the human pair are created last as the crowning accomplishment in God's movement toward creative freedom, in this story adam is created first, and only then is the lush abundance of plants made to grow, followed by the formation of the beasts of the field and the birds of the air. Only after all of that, moreover, does the sexual differentiation of the man and the woman take place in this second account of creation.

We miss the full impact of the second creation story if we force it to conform to the framework of the first. But if we freely use our imagination and listen as children to a story being told in its unfolding, the narrative of creation as here told takes on profound meaning.

Consider the setting as it is described. We are to picture a day "when no plant of the field was yet in the earth and no herb of the field had yet sprung up" (Gen. 2:5). Not only is the earth totally barren, but it is completely dry—no rain had yet fallen and there was no one there to till the ground. This is the setting and the context of God's creating adam: everything barren, dry as dust. We need to keep this picture in mind as the story unfolds.

A mist slowly rises from the earth, and all the ground becomes moistened. The dry dust becomes cohesive and pliable. Now the Lord God, like a potter, is ready to work. He comes down and scoops up the moistened, cohesive dust and begins to mold it together in his skillful hands until it takes on the form of *adam*, the human being. But more is needed. The Lord God breathes his own breath into adam, and the human being becomes a living soul, filled with the breath of God, the breath of life.

Human as you are, too, pause a moment to experience with adam that first breath of life, that initial experience of being alive. How exhilarating! With God's own breath filling him, or you, a response of praise seems appropriate. But as adam, as you, look around, what do you see? Nothing! Nothing but dust, dust moistened by dew. All is empty, barren—there is no other life. What does it all mean? Who am I? What am I here for? What am I supposed to do? How shall I survive? The questions could go on and on, basic questions regarding the meaning of life. In that first moment of life there seem to be only questions with no answers.

Yet the Lord God is already busy providing answers. Off to the east the Lord God is planting a garden called Eden. There he causes to grow "every tree that is pleasant to the sight and good for food" (Gen. 2:9). A river of water flows through the garden and divides into four rivers that flow to the surrounding areas, where there is an abundance of gold—good gold. Other precious metals, bdellium, and onyx stone are found there also. The description of this lush garden and its surroundings seems to go on and on.

Then, the narrative tells us, the Lord God took the human being, adam, whom he had made, and placed him in this lush garden. From total barrenness, emptiness, to this fabulously rich surrounding! What a change! What a contrast! Could adam's (or our) response be anything other than a childlike "WOW!"? Surely adam would experience in this transition some sense of his Creator's full provision for his life, the beginning of an answer to his many questions.

Now at home in the garden, adam receives two messages from his Creator. The first is that adam has a meaningful purpose to fulfill. Adam has been placed in the Garden of Eden "to till it and keep it" (Gen. 2:15). The human being is given a twofold task. Adam is to take care of the garden so that by working the soil and caring for the plants and trees there he will bring forth something new—new trees and plants that produce new fruit. But adam is to till the garden in such a way that at the same time he "keeps" it; he is to preserve what is already there. However different in the telling, the theme is the same as that in the first creation story: out of the existing creation the human being is to bring forth something new in such a way that the old is preserved and enhanced by what is newly produced.

The second message from the Lord God further defines adam's relationship to the garden and to himself. Adam may eat of every tree of the garden except one. To him it is forbidden to eat of the tree of the knowledge of good and evil. Adam may eat of the tree of life in the midst of the garden (vs. 9), but not of the tree of the knowledge of good and evil. As this message defines adam's relationship to the garden, it also defines his relationship to his Creator. Adam is to derive his knowledge of good and evil not from himself but from the Lord God, from the will of his Creator. Within adam's relationship to the Lord God lies the meaning of his life, the source of his breath, the discovery of his purpose, and the experience of his freedom. Within that covenant relationship the tree of life is his freely to enjoy along with the others. Turn away from this relationship with the Lord God, and "you shall die" (Gen. 2:17). Adam experiences the Lord God as his protector who identifies beforehand how his freedom and purpose can either be preserved or be destroyed. His purpose, freedom, and even life itself exist in his relationship to the Lord God. The relationship is one of simple and mutual trust. As adam responds with praise to the source of all goodness, grace, love, and freedom, he will experience all of these qualities expanding and growing within himself. No limits are imposed on adam's growth.

The relationship between adam and the Lord God is entirely the same in this story as it was in Genesis 1. Here, however, the sense of God's full provision for adam's needs seems to be heightened, with a corresponding sense of adam's capacity to respond to the Lord God's provision. Yet up to this point, though we can sense it in our imagination, we do not read of any explicit response from the human being. Could something be muting his response of praise?

Before adam is even aware of it in himself, the Lord God senses his need and identifies that something is "not good." The Lord God understands him and knows his needs better than adam knows himself. The human being is alone, and that, the Lord God knows, is not good. Adam, who has received the breath of life from God's own in-breathing, was created to be in relationship—not just with God, but with others like himself. The image-bearer needs a helper suitable for him, a fellow creature with whom he can enjoy a relationship of mutual trust and growth.

In response to the need he perceives in adam, the Lord God forms out of the ground all the beasts of the field which, unlike the plants and trees of the garden, have the freedom to move about, as adam can. The Lord God thus continues to multiply his own full provision for adam's life. And adam responds my naming the cattle, the birds, and the beasts as they are all brought to him. But in the naming of them adam experiences himself as having dominion over them, and as therefore distant from them. Each has its own being, to be named and thus experienced according to its own identity. But none is suitable as a companion for the human being. Even with animals below and with God above, adam is still alone.

And so from out of the human being's own flesh the Lord God now separates out another. While adam sleeps, the Lord God fashions from his side another who is truly like adam, and yet so very different! The one newly formed is brought to adam as "woman" (Gen. 2:22). Now his sense of exultation can no longer be held back. God's full provision for human life is complete!

Adam's song of praise contains two themes. First, this new creation is one with me: "This at last is bone of my bone and flesh of my flesh" (Gen. 2:23). He glories—yes, revels—first of all in his recognition of her oneness with him. The woman whom the Lord God fashioned from his own being and brought to him is not beneath him but is one with him. Secondly, adam's glorying contains a recognition of this new creature as being different from himself. He recognizes her as *ishah*, woman, who was taken out of *ish*, or man as masculine. He does not need to name her as he named the animals; he can only recognize her for who she is and acclaim both her oneness with him and her separateness from him. And as he recognizes her simultaneous oneness and otherness, he also comes to a new awareness of himself, the awareness of himself as *ish*, as male. Before this, the first human being was simply adam, the human being, undifferentiated as to gender or sexual awareness. He only comes to know himself as sexual, as masculine, through the presence before him of one who is separated out from him as feminine while still being one with him. In their separateness and their union, they will each discover the possibilities of freedom and growth, possibilities inherent in their "being-in-relationship."

However different the telling of the two creation stories, the message is one and the same: God creates, and out of the existing creation he separates a new and greater creation, which in its newness enhances the identity of the earlier creation; as a new unity is formed between the new and the old, the union itself enhances each of them within the new relationship.

Adam, the human being whom God created in his own image, is both male and female—one, and yet two. Out of the two comes something new, a relationship in which they can be fully naked, fully open to each other without shame or fear. Theirs is a relationship of simple trust. Theirs is a relationship much like that within the being of God himself who is one God, yet distinctly Father, Son, and

Spirit. And it is a relationship not unlike that of God to his creation and to his image-bearer, a relationship of trust which offers the freedom for continually growing in self-awareness and in awareness of the other. In their union each continually becomes something more than before, and that process is to continue throughout the generations as new separations or "leavings" create new unions or "cleavings" which promote further growth. That is the meaning of love, and of the freedom to love.

Human freedom flourishes only within a circle of trust and love, in a relationship in which each values the other, a relationship which does not restrict but enhances the distinct being and identity of each.

But what if a separation would occur which seeks not a greater whole, but instead restricts human responsivity? What would that do to human freedom?

3

WHAT'S WRONG WITH BEING RIGHT?

Responsivity in the Fall

The story of the fall into sin narrates the dramatic interplay between God's sovereignty and our human responsivity. Eventually all of creation is drawn into the drama, first with the serpent, then with the ground and its produce, and finally with the Garden of Eden and its tree of life.

The Drama of the Fall

The serpent in Genesis 3 is described at the outset as the most subtle—crafty—of all the wild creatures God has made. Subtly he asks the human pair about what God has said. Has he really said that they were not to eat of any tree of the garden? The serpent, we should note, is not lying here; he is asking a question, checking things out, as it were. So far he has done no wrong.

The woman responds appropriately. She reports accurately just what God had said was permissible to eat and what he had warned against, including the consequence of dying if they should eat of the tree in the middle of the garden. Does she subtly exaggerate and thus already distort the prohibition when she adds that they are not even to *touch* the tree? Or is this addition a wise insight on her part, in that she perceives that the very reaching out to touch what is forbidden would already violate the spirit, if not the letter, of what God has said?

Where is the man when all this is happening? In one version (NIV) he seems to be right there at her side but saying nothing. "She also gave some to her husband, who was with her, and he ate it" (Gen. 3:6). Is he a passive, unassertive male who lets his wife make all the decisions? Or is he, in self-assured confidence, quietly being supportive of her ability to assert and handle herself as well as anyone? Could this reaction be his recognition that she is as qualified as he to respond to the serpent and to exercise the dominion given to them together over all of earth's creatures?

The serpent makes four assertions about the consequences of eating the forbidden fruit:

1. You will not die.
2. Your eyes will be opened.
3. You will be like God, knowing good and evil.
4. And God himself knows all this to be true.

On all four counts, once again, the serpent is right. He is not lying. For when the man and the woman eat, they do not immediately die; their eyes are actually opened (Gen. 3:7), and they do become like God in knowing good and evil (vs. 22). (And the serpent is quite right in saying that God knows that all this is true.) So the woman and the man believe and act together on truth when they take the fruit of the tree and eat of it. What they ate was not rotten or toxic; it was "good for food, and...a delight to the eye" (Gen. 3:6).

So far the serpent is right, and the woman and man are acting on the basis of that reality. So the question seems appropriate: What's wrong with being right? How can eating what is good be bad?

Being Right vs. Trusting

Note that up to this time the question of being right was never an issue. The man and woman were able–naively, we might think–to rely on God's full provision for their lives. Theirs was simply a relationship of trust. They experienced their Creator as the source of all goodness to them. They knew him as one who trusted them to till and keep the garden. He entrusted to them dominion over all the birds, fish, and beasts. They experienced their provider as one who would expand and enhance their lives from out of his own fullness as they lived out of their relationship to him.

In this atmosphere of trust the man and woman were enabled freely to experience their mutual nakedness without shame, without concern over one or the other being right or wrong, and without one trying to gain advantage over the other. They experienced God's sovereignty as a source of empowerment and freedom, and in trust they responded with thankfulness and praise. They were familiar with the sound of the Lord God as he walked in the garden in the cool of the day (3:8). They recognized his presence immediately. A sense of shared intimacy not only between the man and the woman, but also between God and the two of them seems to be presupposed here and to permeate the story. Their relationships—to each other, to the rest of the creation, and to God—had given their lives meaning, worth, and freedom. They were finite creatures vastly different from the Lord God, but they were created to live with him in a union of trust that would magnify his name and enhance their lives. Within this circle of trust there had been a total sense of belonging in which the issue of "being right" did not arise.

To shift the main concern of life away from trusting to that of being right is the essence of the serpent's temptation. By eating the forbidden fruit the human pair yield to the tempting vision of being right instead of trusting. They discover the burden of being "like God, knowing good and evil."

Knowing Good and Evil

How, we may ask, does God know good and evil? To begin with, we can say that God knows good and evil experientially. He knows good as the expression of his own sovereign good pleasure in creating, and he "knows" evil from his experience of the rebellion of and ensuing conflict with Lucifer. In a similar way, as the man and woman eat of the forbidden fruit, they gain a new experience of evil as well as a new and contrasting awareness of what is good.

Moreover, God knows himself as the source or fountain of all that is good. Note that James, in his New Testament epistle, has this sense of God when he writes: "Every good endowment and every perfect gift is from above, coming down from the Father of lights.... Of his own will he brought us forth by the word of truth" (1:17-18). Anything that originates outside of and against God's self is evil.

Not only is the Lord God the source of all goodness and truth, but his will is also the *measure* of what is good and what is evil. What is in accordance with God's will is good; what is contrary to God's will is evil, for God is sovereign.

The human pair now begin to know good and evil in themselves as God knows it. By eating fruit from the tree of the knowledge of good and evil, the woman is now making *her* experience, her will, and her desire the measure of what is good; evil is now determined to be what is contrary to *her* will. And the man now likewise makes *his* experience and will and desire the measure of what is good; evil for him is now determined to be what is contrary to *his* will.

Trust breaks down when each one makes herself or himself the measure of what is good. Where trust breaks down, fear fills the vacuum. In the drama of the fall, three behaviors result from fear. First, the man and the woman hide themselves from God just as they hide from each other behind their fig leaves; each has become an individual in isolation. Second, each begins to blame another; each sets self up as judge. Third, one relates to the other by controlling or trying to change the other; the curse results in their turning dominion into a human power struggle.

A New Freedom: Individualism

The man and woman have now each become like God in knowing good and evil. In this likeness to God they experience a new freedom—a freedom which separates them from God and from each other, leading them to hide from God and from each other. Here is a separation which has no power to reflect glory back to God, as did the other separations at the various stages of creation. This freedom to separate, to individuate, has no potential for a union which will enhance the identity of both in a newly formed whole. It is a freedom that is grasped outside the relationship of trust that had existed between a sovereign God and a responsive creature; the freedom of individualism is a freedom that focuses inwardly upon oneself, breaking out of the circle of love where freedom finds its true home.

As this freedom drives a separation between the man and the woman, each making himself/herself the measure of what is good and what is evil, they are now competing with each other over who determines what is good or evil, just as they are each competing with God. Not only is the circle of love with God broken, but the circle of love between the man and the woman is broken also. His freedom now becomes the freedom to pursue and serve his own needs and wishes without regard for God or for any other being. Likewise, her freedom is now the freedom to pursue her own wishes and needs alone. Freedom has thus become an end in itself, an individual trait in isolation from the relationships of life and love. It is a trait that stands in opposition to relationships, whether with God or with others.

Moreover, the resulting isolation and competition make each one vulnerable to the power exercised by the other. His freedom and power threaten and limit her freedom and power, as hers do his. The man and the woman can no longer be naked and unashamed, completely open and trusting with each other. Each has become the judge over the other. They hide themselves from each other's gaze by sewing fig leaves to cover themselves. Since each is now in his and her own eyes the measure of what is good and right, the differences between them are no longer a source of pure delight that enrich them both. Instead, those differences become a potential threat to each of them. They have lost the freedom which enables an endless discovery of life and love, of trust and joy and praise within a covenant union with God. In its place the human pair experience a new freedom in isolation from and competition with each other and God, a freedom that produces distrust and fear.

Freedom in isolation and competition makes the human pair vulnerable also to the power of the Lord God. As they hear the sound of the Lord God walking in the garden in the cool of the day, they immediately hide themselves from God as well. Now God's sovereign power is experienced as a threat to their new independence. (Does the exercise of this new freedom apart from their relationship to the Lord God now limit the sovereignty of God? Is this the source of the never-resolved tension between human freedom and divine sovereignty?)

God calls them to responsibility–accountability. In response to God's call, "Where are you?" they emerge from their hiding place and acknowledge their fear (Gen. 3:10). Fear has replaced trust as they hide from a seeking God and from each other. That fear will eventually become a dominant motif permeating all of human life.

A New Responsiveness: Blaming

The new freedom which the man and woman claim for themselves brings with it a new form of responding to God's questioning. The man now exercises his profoundly altered responsivity by pointing to the woman, identifying her as the one God had given him, in effect saying, "She gave it to me–it's really her fault, if not ultimately yours, God." And the man was right. God had given her to him. And she had given him the fruit to eat. It was her fault. She was to blame. The man was right about that.

God seems to side with him. God immediately turns to the woman, who expresses her responsivity by pointing to the serpent who beguiled her. And she, too, in blaming the serpent, was quite right. It was the serpent's doing, the snake's fault. The woman was right about that. Even God does not dispute that she is right. The Lord God turns to curse the serpent on the spot.

Yet there is something wrong, radically wrong, with their each being right, just as there was something very wrong in all the right and truth that the serpent had spoken earlier. The questions at issue here are these: How do the right and the truth spoken here actually function? What purpose do they serve?

The man is right in blaming the woman, but focusing on this rightful blame serves only to evade what part his own responses played in his eating. The woman is right in blaming the serpent, but focusing on this rightful blaming only serves to avoid what part her own responses played in her eating. The serpent, too, was right in all that it said about their eating the tempting fruit. But all of the serpent's "right talk" was divorced from the covenant relationship of love and trust between God and the human pair.

The serpent's "right talk" had nothing to do with what would promote the life and growth of those involved. "Right talk" was divorced from "love talk" and "trust talk." That is what is wrong with being right. This new form of responsiveness limits, even destroys, the potential of relationships to promote the growth of trust and love. Truth and right expressed outside a relationship of mutual love and trust become deceitful and destructive of life and growth precisely in their appeal as truth and right.

A New Dominion: Controlling

The dominion which the man and woman shared together at the dawn of creation they now begin to turn against each other. The curse which follows from their fateful freedom turns the dominion that was enhancing to each into a struggle for control that sets each against the other. The one who is physically the smaller and weaker now becomes subject to him who is larger and stronger. Each now assumes roles that restrict rather than enlarge and enhance their responsiveness to each other and to God.

Even the earth itself seems to respond with a new power gone wild, inducing a kind of power struggle between man and nature. The earth produces noxious plants, thorns, and thistles which, rather than enhancing either the earth or the human pair, increase the sweat and pain of the struggle for survival.

As if to fulfill the curse at once, the man takes it upon himself to name the woman who is his wife, as earlier he had named the animals below him and defined their being. He gives to her the name "Eve" which is said to mean "Mother of all living." He thus defines and thereby limits her being and her role by her biological function of bearing children. That role now defines her identity, at least in his eyes. His relationship to her has thus altered radically. No longer is he there to celebrate the oneness and the differences together in such a way that her identity is enhanced and grows through his, and his through hers. He now restricts her identity and role according to his own image of what is right and good—a vision far more limited than God's original imagining. And she accepts that restriction as her lot, thereby escaping her responsibilities for exercising dominion with him. He now appropriates the name "Adam," human being, to himself. As she is now "Eve," he alone becomes "Adam" who exercises by himself dominion over all the other creatures, including now his little Eve.

The Essence of Sin

When we seek to identify the essence of sin we are looking for some way to recognize not just what that original sin was all about, but what characterizes our own sin, as well. What is there in that original sin that we are also prone to reenact in countless ways?

Sin in its essence has variously been identified as pride, as a missing of the mark, as a transgression of God's law, as disobedience to God. And each of these is a valid description of sin. Yet of each of these we may still ask, what is its essence? What is the essence of pride, of missing the mark, of transgression, of disobedience?

Furthermore, each of these definitions gives sin a bad name right at the outset. We may speak at times of a healthy pride, but we also know what sinful pride looks like, and want to avoid it. And who of us would say, "I really like to miss the mark," or, "I delight in transgressing God's law," or, "Disobedience to God makes my day"? Actually, few of us take open delight in blatant defiance of God and his laws. What tempts us is sin that looks attractive, enticing, desirable, good, right, and even able to make us wise. That is exactly how sin is portrayed in the Genesis story of the fall: "God knows that when you eat of it your eyes will be opened, and you will be like God, knowing good and evil" (Gen. 3:5). You will become wise and free! That's something any of us could easily fall for!

How attractive it is for us image-bearers to be invited to be "like God." It even has a pious ring to it. And what can be wrong with wanting to know good and evil as God does? How desirable it appears to be to have the knowledge of good and evil within ourselves! And how seductive it is to think of ourselves—our ideas, insights, feelings, needs, intentions, and faith—as being the measure of what is good and right! Here we discover a meaning for "sin" that underlies those other meanings: pride, missing the mark, transgression, and disobedience. These all have to do with *making oneself the measure of what is good and right.*

Whenever we focus on the importance of our being right and good we distinguish ourselves from others whom we "know" to be wrong and bad. But isn't it better to be right than wrong, to be on the side of good rather than of evil? I rather like thinking that I am right and others wrong—something I find ample opportunity for and find considerable truth in as well. And I feel quite virtuous when I know that I am good where others have been bad or morally evil. There's something exhilarating in making myself, consciously or unconsciously, the measure of what is right and good. That's what underlies all sinful pride. That's what is involved in our missing the mark, in our transgressing God's law, and in our disobeying God.

The essence of sin involves, first of all, choosing what is inherently good but is grasped in such a way that it undermines relationships of trust and love. Secondly, the essence of sin lies in our making ourselves the measure of right and good. This explains why sin is so attractive, and why all of us can so easily justify or rationalize our own sin. There is usually something good or right or true found in the sin we fall for. What is wrong with a focus on our being right and good, even when there is truth in our claim, is that such a focus removes us from the circle of trust and love, whether with God or with one another. When we become preoccupied with our being right or good we severely limit our responsive capacity to be trusting and loving.

The Consequences of Sin

Fear

The immediate consequence of making ourselves the measure of right and good is that we become afraid. Fear is the first human emotion that is directly expressed and owned in the Scriptures, and fear is one of the most potent forces underlying much of human behavior that is destructive. Fear, the opposite of trust, is a response that limits our capacity to respond freely to other human beings, to the rest of creation, and to God himself.

Hiding

Because of fear we hide ourselves from one another and from God, as did the man and woman in the garden. The fig leaves behind which we hide are a wonderfully ambivalent symbol of where much of human life is lived, a symbol of all the barriers, the walls, the masks that come between us and others, even between ourselves and those we love most. The fig leaves symbolize all that is wrong with human life: fear that destroys the very intimacy we crave, avoidance of the openness we so much desire, practice of the pretenses we all hate.

At the same time, the fig leaves are also a symbol of what we need in order to survive. They are a form of protection for our vulnerability. If the fig leaves are a symbol of all that is wrong with human life, of all that needs to be overcome or removed if we are to grow, they are just as truly a symbol of the respect we need to observe for another's selfhood and privacy, and for our own self as well. Intrusively to tear away another's defenses would be a form of rape. In the Genesis story God himself reinforces the meaning of the fig leaves by providing animal skins to cover the man and the woman more completely. The fig leaves and the animal skins symbolize both the curse of restricted responsiveness and the blessing of a continued protection that enables life to go on in postponement of death.

Blaming

In blaming we seek to maintain our own right by highlighting the wrong in the other and thereby diminishing his or her stature. It doesn't matter whether the blaming is right or wrong, justified or not. Even when it is justified, blaming or judging restricts the potential of the other person's responsiveness. It invites defensiveness and restricts one's capacity to respond to the other with any understanding or empathy that could result in growth for both parties. When one experiences being blamed it becomes difficult to respond with the warmth and gratitude that enhances a relationship. The paradox of sin, thus, is that it introduces new kinds of responses that have the effect of diminishing our responsivity.

Controlling

The drive to control, dominate, manipulate another was not present before the fall. Adam's naming and thereby controlling the woman as Eve is reenacted over and over again in our world, not only by men over women, but in one form or another in all of human relationships. When we act in controlling ways toward others we restrict rather than enhance their potential for growth. At the same time our own capacity for growth through relationships becomes more rigidly limited.

The Naming of Sin

Original Sin

All sin can be viewed as a reenactment of the original sin. When we confess the doctrine of original sin we are not blaming Adam and Eve for our sinning, nor ourselves for their sin. What we are doing is acknowledging that we participate in or reenact theirs. Each of us is born into a world of broken trust, and we each perpetuate the brokenness. We succumb to the temptations to make ourselves, our wills, our desires, our needs, our insights, our vision, or our faith the measure of what is right and good. Fear is the inevitable result, along with shame. We respond to each other by hiding ourselves, by withdrawing from each other when hurt or angry or afraid. We easily blame and judge each other, driving a further wedge between us, and we take it upon ourselves to control or change or manipulate each other. All of these typical, everyday responses limit our capacity to grow. Our responsivity–the trait that makes us most like God and therefore endows us with an infinite capacity freely to grow through all our relationships–becomes rigidified. Instead of growing, we are dying from our participation in sin.

Total Depravity

When we make ourselves the measure of what is right, and when fear encourages us to avoid, blame, or control others, our responsivity is constricted. This process reaches into and affects all areas of human life. In no area of our lives are we as responsive to God and to others as we could be and as God intended us to be. That is the simple but profound truth in the Reformation doctrine of "total depravity." This doctrine is frequently and mistakenly characterized as saying that we are as evil as we could possibly be, with nothing good left within us. Far from being that, it is a recognition of how sin alters our responsivity in every area of our lives. Eventually we may also discover something immensely freeing in this perspective (cf. chapter 5).

Responsivity and Sovereignty

What has happened to human responsivity and freedom in relationship to divine sovereignty as a result of the fall? As our responsivity atrophies through a focus on our being right or good, we lose dimensions of our freedom. To be sure, sin introduces a new kind of freedom, but it is a freedom that ends up destroying trust and undermining the building of a community of love, eroding the sense of belonging. It is a freedom that is divorced from the responsiveness of love because of its focus on the individual and his or her needs, desires, goals, and happiness. One person's or one group's pursuit of freedom often results in hurt, bondage, or death for others. Pursuing our own freedom in that way, we lose our capacity to respond to others in any way that produces growth for them or for ourselves. The true freedom, the freedom to grow, for which we were created, is lost when our concern focuses on our being right or good in contrast to others.

Our narrowed responsivity, our focusing on our own individual right or good, results in fragmented responsibility. Instead of being freely responsive to God and to others, we have to take on duties and obligations. We feel guilty and blameworthy. Held accountable for our moral choices, we are forced to assume the consequences for our actions. Yet our moral choices easily stray far from the covenant relationship between an all-providing Creator and a responsive image-bearer. They are now made in human isolation, in consideration of ourselves alone. Outside the divinely established circle of trust, we have only ourselves to draw on in making our moral decisions and in growing toward maturity. However well we exercise our responsibility in any of its many meanings, we are doing so outside a relationship to divine love and goodness. The freedom in which we exercise that responsibility is also the freedom that turns away from God and to ourselves as the measure of what is right.

Christian theology has always held that such human freedom is insufficient to bring us back to God. Reformed theology has always insisted that such freedom is totally incapable of playing any role at all in turning us back to God. And that is tantamount to saying that we have lost the freedom we once had–freedom to turn to God and live in union with him. We are, as the apostle Paul says bluntly, dead (cf. Eph. 2:1).

In all of our theological reflections we need to keep in mind, for the sake of clarity, that we are dealing with two very different kinds of freedom. The first kind of freedom is that which is ours from creation, and which is experienced only within the relationship between responsive image-bearers and their all-providing Creator whose powerful goodness, love, and grace are experienced as the never-exhausted fountain of all goodness. Within this divine-human circle of trust the potential for human growth is endless. This is the freedom that was lost through the fall into sin. (But the wonder of God's grace is that this freedom is still available to all of us, as we shall discuss further in chapters 4 and 5.)

The second kind of freedom, the freedom to become like God in making *ourselves* the measure of all good, is a freedom we possess from, and since, the fall. This second kind of freedom was not a part of our relationship to God in the beginning, but was grasped or discovered in the fall. This is a freedom that seemed to make one wise as well as free, but turned out to be a wisdom leading only to self-destruction. What essentially characterizes this new freedom is that it is self-limiting and even self-destructive, as it introduces an infinite variety of power struggles among human beings. This is the freedom that sets me against you, us against them, and all of us together against God. This freedom is what Paul in Romans 8 calls the "mind [set on] the flesh," which, in terms of our discussion here, could be called the mind focused on one's own right and good. This is the mind or the freedom that cannot please God. Salvation will never come through the exercise of this kind of freedom.

In summary, as we watched the unfolding of creation we saw separations occurring that enriched both what already existed and what was newly created, as the new and the old together each time formed a new whole. And each new whole was good, glorifying God's being. In the fall, however, a very different kind of separation occurred. Instead of enhancing human life and all of creation, a separation occurred that was limiting, diminishing human responsivity. It was a separation which also robbed the Creator God of his glory.

Will God himself in his sovereign and overflowing grace find a way to overcome this evil? Will he turn even this self-destructive separation to his own glory and to the further enhancement of his creation and his image-bearer? A hint of God's response is found within the curse pronounced on the serpent (Gen. 3:15). A foreshadowing of something new is found in the promised triumph of the woman's seed over the serpent's seed, pointing us to a new way of doing right which is found in the story of God's redemption.

4

WHAT'S RIGHT IN A WORLD GONE WRONG?

Responsivity in Redemption

The correlation is broken. The circle of love has been ruptured. Human responsiveness has become fragmented into ever smaller disconnected pieces of "responsibility."

How can what is broken be restored? How can what has been ruptured be healed? How can what has become fragmented be enlarged and made whole again? Can all the King's horses and all the King's men put Humpty Dumpty together again?

In creation, the responsive capacity of the creature expanded as each new act of creation produced a separation which enhanced the new and the old alike within a newly formed relationship. Each new whole magnified the glory of the sovereign God. The covenant relationship between a sovereign God and a responsive image-bearer had the potential for unlimited, never-ending growth. The fall, however, brings a separation, and a freedom that breaks away from the circle of divine and human love, resulting in a responsiveness that is ever more limited and restricted as each individual self becomes the measure of what is right and good. The movement of life turns away from expansive growth toward a diminution that ends in death. And God is robbed of his glory.

In such a world, where all has gone so wrong, Christian faith proclaims that "in Christ God was reconciling the world to himself" (II Corinthians 5:19). The relationship is restored. The rupture is being healed. What was fragmented is being made whole again. The fruitless, self-restricting freedom and separation inherent in sin is overcome and turned into a new union with God which restores and enhances the potential of human responsiveness and growth beyond measuring (I John 3:2). And God's glory is not diminished, but is magnified—also beyond measuring (Ephesians 2:7; 3:18-21; Romans 11:33-36). What brings about this change?

Two Views of What's Right

In a world gone wrong, how are things set right? How does God restore right to our world? What is "right" for us in a world gone wrong? These are questions concerning redemption that are worth reflecting on again and again, as the church has done for centuries. What is the significance of the life, death, and resurrection of Jesus of Nazareth? What has Christ accomplished? The varied answers to these questions fall broadly into one of two categories: Either Jesus brings a revelation from God with the possibility of change for us, or he himself brings about an actual change.

In the first category of views God in Christ fully reveals what he is really like. The significance of Christ's person and work lies in his disclosure of the heart of God; in Christ we learn that God is a God of love, forgiveness, reconciliation, and peace; God wants and indeed invites all of us back into the circle of his love. Christ also discloses what we on our part must do for that to occur, but nothing is really changed until or unless we believe. We must first respond with our individual acts or decisions of faith. Our act of faith, with our love, restores the relationship between God and ourselves. By our faith we make complete the circle of love with God. What God in Christ does is to reveal or create the possibility of restoration; what we do in faith makes that possibility an actuality.

That, in one form or another, is the viewpoint of Pelagianism, Roman Catholicism, Arminianism, classic liberalism, fundamentalism, and other forms of pietism. However different these various viewpoints are, they have in common a sense that whatever it is that God has done, no real change occurs until we do our part. These varying viewpoints may contend among themselves over what our part is; our part may involve moral or social actions, or participation in the sacraments, or making a decision for Christ, or something else, but in one way or another *we must do something right ourselves* before the significant change involved in reconciliation actually occurs. And if we fail to keep on "doing something right," we lose our salvation or fall from grace or out of fellowship with God.

In the other category of views the self-disclosure of God in Christ is also prominent, but what is revealed is a change that has already taken place. Here Christ himself brings about all the change that needs doing. Reconciliation is already an accomplished reality through the birth, life, death, and resurrection of Jesus Christ. Our believing adds nothing to that change—except our response of confession, praise, adoration, and thanksgiving. Our calling is to live in the new kingdom of God that has actually come, and to live out of the restored responsiveness that is now ours.

With some variations, this is the Augustinian approach of Luther and Calvin. This viewpoint comes to expression, for example, in Calvin's commentary on John 13:31.

> In all the creatures, indeed, both high and low, the glory of God shines, but nowhere has it shown more brightly than in the cross, in which there has been an astonishing change of things, the condemnation of all men has been manifested, sin has been blotted out, salvation has been restored to men; and, in short, the whole world has been renewed, and everything restored to good order. (John Calvin 1509-1564)

For Calvin reconciliation, salvation, the blotting out of sin, the renewal of the world, the restoration of everything to good order—the whole "astonishing change"—does not occur with our believing but was a "done deal" in Christ's redemptive work.

In each of the viewpoints under the first category, the new "right" that restores the covenant relationship between us and God is something, in the final analysis, that we do; our doing the "right" thing is what makes the difference between those of us who enter the kingdom of God and those who are left out or cast out. In the perspective of the Reformation of Luther and Calvin, however, the new "right" is not something we do at all, but is wholly God's way of setting things right.

One irony of church history is that both the movement of

Lutheranism and that of Calvinism soon began to focus more and more on who had the right view of justification by faith alone. Lutherans and Calvinists began to contend with each other over who of them had the right view of how the divine attributes relate to the human nature of Christ and of how Christ is present to us in the Eucharist. Each also insisted on their own "right" over against the wrong of the papists and the wrong of the Anabapists. As a consequence, Lutherans in their way, and Calvinists in theirs, quickly joined all the other movements of church history in attempting to determine what is the "right" that we must do and hold on to if we are to be united with God in reconciliation and live together within the same church fellowship. As in the original sin, so also in doing theology, when we begin to focus on our own right doing, we lose or narrow our capacity to live responsively in a loving relationship with others.

The Substitutionary Atonement

The doctrine of the substitutionary atonement is a good example of the same tendency. This doctrine is itself a response of faith to the message of Christ's death on the cross. As such, the doctrine of the substitutionary atonement makes clear that Christ secures reconciliation by what he does: he gives himself as a sacrifice for us. He is our substitute. He takes on himself the punishment for our sins so that we need never bear the wrath of God against sin ourselves. What is more, the sinlessness of Christ, his righteousness, is "imputed" to us, so that despite all our sin we are accounted wholly righteous before God as if we had never sinned.

The doctrine of the substitutionary atonement is clear and relatively easy to grasp and remember, and it calls us to a response of trust in God and confidence in his forgiveness as we live our lives. Faced with our own sin and with all the fears that are evoked by it, we learn from this doctrine to turn our focus away from ourselves—away from what we have done right or wrong—to the reality that God has set things right in his own way. We learn that we really can trust God's way.

However, as an explanation of God's way of doing right in a world gone wrong, this doctrine can give rise to any number of questions and objections. Is the whole matter of redemption really just a legal transaction, one founded on the grand legal fiction that the guilty are legally declared innocent and the innocent one is legally declared guilty? Was Jesus literally punished by God? Does God's wrath need to be appeased by a blood sacrifice before he can enter a love relationship with us?

The very fact that objections can be raised to the idea of substitutionary atonement leads to a defense of this doctrine against its detractors. In this way our focus subtly but surely shifts once again to that of making certain that we have the right understanding of the doctrine of atonement, in contrast to those who have the wrong understanding. The focus of our faith turns inward upon ourselves to our "right" over against someone else's "wrong." Our right understanding of this doctrine then becomes the measure by which we judge the validity of another's Christianity or faith. Our believing in the substitutionary atonement becomes the "something right" that we must do to be in good standing with God–or at least with the church. And the very atonement which brought reconciliation becomes divisive in our hands.

Instead of asking whether this doctrine is "right" or "wrong," true or false, we would do better to ask: What is it in this doctrine that expresses the faith response that we can have toward God? How does it help us to trust in him as we live out our brief and uncertain lives? Or, what might be this doctrine's limitations in expressing our faith? In this way we keep the focus of our belief on the God in whom we trust, instead of yielding to the temptation to shift the focus to proving that we are right while others are wrong.

One of the problems with making the doctrine of the substitutionary atonement the central one in Christology is that it tends to put the focus of Christ's reconciling work on his dying rather than on his living. His living seems to have importance primarily insofar as it demonstrates his being without sin, a precondition for a valid sacrificial atonement. Beyond that, his living, his innocence, and his righteousness are not themselves seen as an integral part of the reconciliation that God was working out in Christ. They are only preliminary to his real work of dying.

In Romans Paul does speak of God putting Christ Jesus forward as "an expiation by his blood" (3:25), and of our being "now justified by his blood" (5:9) and thus surely being "saved by him from the wrath of God" (5:9); as enemies "we were reconciled to God by the death of his Son" (5:10). The significance of Jesus' death is not to be minimized. Yet Jesus' death on the cross is the culmination of his life. His dying, with the shedding of his blood, is the apex of his life as a life of obedience and righteousness. He emptied himself, became a servant, and was obedient—even to the extent of death on a cross (Phil. 2:7-8). In the same context that Paul speaks of being reconciled by his death, he speaks of how "much more" we shall be "saved by his life" (Rom. 5:10).

As Paul goes on in Romans 5 to extol Christ over Adam, he does not once refer to the death of Christ. Instead he writes of "the grace of God and the free gift in the grace of that one man Jesus Christ" (5:15), and of "the abundance of grace and the free gift of righteousness" that comes "through the one man Jesus Christ" (5:17). Paul points to "one man's act of righteousness" that leads to acquittal (5:18), and to "one man's obedience" (5:19). Paul sums up the contrast between Christ and Adam by saying that "as sin reigned in death," so through Christ Jesus "grace also... might reign through righteousness to eternal life" (5:21). Paul's primary focus lies in the whole person of Christ who embodied the righteousness of God, and did so all through his life to the very end. The blood of the cross is redemptive because it expresses the full extent of the righteousness embodied in the life of Jesus.

In the Hebrew perspective, blood represents the flow of life (Gen. 9:4ff). Thus reference to Jesus' shed blood inherently refers to the full life of Christ from its beginning to his dying end. What changes, renews, and restores the world to God is not an isolated act of physical bleeding or even dying. What brings reconciliation is a new righteousness, a new way of doing right that goes all the way—even to the cursed cross. In a world gone wrong, God himself provides this new righteousness, this new way of "doing right."

The Kingdom and its Righteousness

Paul's Letter to the Romans

From the beginning of his letter to the Romans, Paul makes clear that the power of the gospel lies in its revealing "the righteousness of God" (Rom. 1:16-17). These verses express the theme that unfolds through the entire letter: God's righteousness rather than our own is the way to redemption. The remainder of chapter 1 refers to various forms of our *un*righteousness; chapters 2 through 3:30 detail the inadequacy of our way of doing right through keeping the law.

In contrast to our way of doing right Paul sets forth in chapter 3:21ff. a wholly new and different form of right, to which the law and prophets bear witness, but which is embodied in Christ. Christ is "put forward as an expiation" or atonement, which was "to show God's righteousness" (3:25), and to demonstrate "that he himself is righteous" (3:26). As Paul characterizes this new righteousness that is from God, he speaks of it as a "free gift" and as "the abundance of grace" (5:17). What God does right in Christ is to embrace sinners with his love—even to the point of death (5:8, 10). God's righteousness and God's grace are intimately related. They are, in fact, one and the same.

The contrast between the two ways of righteousness that form the theme of this entire letter comes to direct expression again in Romans 10:3. "For, being ignorant of the righteousness that comes from God, and seeking to establish their own, they did not submit to God's righteousness." The contrast here comes to expression in the middle of chapters 9-11, which are considered to be Paul's major discourse on the doctrine of election or predestination. What Paul says about election, however, is not a distinct new "doctrine." It is, rather, a further way in which Paul gives expression to his one major theme: a new righteousness has come—not from man, nor from the law, but wholly from God. God's righteousness and divine election are intimately related also. They, too, are one and the same.

One thing is clear about this new righteousness which is from God and is manifested in Christ's whole life, even to his death: through faith we actually participate in and follow this new way of righteousness. It is not merely "imputed" to us in a legal manner. In his way of doing right, God so embraces us with his love and grace that we become joined in a new union with him. We die and live with Christ in this new righteousness. To Paul it is absolutely inconceivable that we who believe in and are united with Christ would not live out of this new righteousness but would choose instead the old way of doing our own "right" that leads to slavery and death (cf. chapter 6).

As Paul shifts our focus away from our doing right to our participating in what God does right, what he puts forth is parallel to what Jesus said in the Sermon on the Mount: all judging (Romans 2:1, 14:10-13; cf. Matthew 7:1-5) and boasting (Rom. 3:19, 27; 11:18, 20, 25; 12:3; cf. Matt. 6:1-18) on our part comes out of the old righteousness. The opposite response of blessing instead of cursing one's persecutors, (Rom. 12:17-21; cf. Matt. 5:10-11), of feeding instead of taking vengeance on an enemy (Rom 12:17-21; cf. Matt. 5:38-48) becomes possible. This is a righteousness that works toward reconciliation–first of all *in* us, and then *through* us. (In the remainder of the book of Romans Paul elaborates on what this new righteousness involves for us.)

It may be an exaggeration to say that Romans is a commentary on the Sermon on the Mount, but it is no exaggeration to suggest that the major themes of the two are so similar that Paul surely had the Sermon on the Mount in mind, if not before him, as he wrote this letter to the Christians in Rome. The central theme of the Sermon on the Mount, a new righteousness, is the very same as that developed by Paul in the book of Romans.

The Sermon on the Mount

The Sermon on the Mount can well be called the "manifesto" of the kingdom of heaven that Jesus came to proclaim. It comes at the beginning of his public ministry, when he first began teaching and "preaching the gospel of the kingdom and healing every disease and every infirmity among the people" (Matt. 4:23).

The unifying theme of this sermon is the righteousness of the kingdom. As he expounds on this theme Jesus is repeatedly contrasting the righteousness of the kingdom with that of the Pharisees and the scribes. Before referring to the commandments regarding murder and adultery, for instance, he says: "For I tell you that unless your righteousness exceeds that of the scribes and Pharisees, you will never enter the kingdom of heaven" (Matt. 5:20). This has to be one of the most startling statements Jesus ever made. I cannot help picturing Jesus with a twinkle in his eye as he made this remark. The common people to whom he spoke looked up to their leaders as being exceptionally righteous. The ordinary folk who heard Jesus talk knew that they could not possibly come anywhere near the level of righteousness that the Pharisees practiced. And here is Jesus telling them that their righteousness must exceed that of the scribes and Pharisees if they are to reach even the entryway to the kingdom of heaven!

The same contrast is implied in the other references to the righteousness of the kingdom. When Jesus says we are to seek first God's kingdom and his righteousness, he again seems to be contrasting this righteousness with that of the rulers of the Jews. And when he calls his disciples to "be perfect as your heavenly Father is perfect" (Matt. 5:48), he is again contrasting the Father's way of being perfect, his way of making things right or whole, with that of the Pharisees. That same contrast of two very different ways of righteousness is evident in all those sayings of chapter 5 which contain the formula: "You have heard that it was said…, but I say unto you" (5:21-48). Surely these sayings are intended to break through the rationalized self-righteous denial of sin in ourselves and to lead the best of us to confession—much like Paul does in chapters 2-3 of Romans.

In considering what characterized the righteousness of the Pharisees, we do well not to caricature them, but to begin by picturing them in the best possible light. After all, their endeavor was foremost a reformation movement, an undertaking that sought renewal among God's people. They wanted Jewish religion to be distinctive in the world, and they wanted its implications to reach into all areas of life every day of the week rather than applying only to Sabbath matters. People who relish down-to-earth, practical kinds of sermons that tell them just how to live their lives in specific ways would have loved to listen to the Pharisees speak. The Pharisees spelled out the right way to live and practice religion as clearly as anyone has ever done. And for the most part they themselves practiced what they preached. They were really not so very different from those of us who are religious leaders today.

So what was it that characterized their "righteousness?" Jesus, of course, saw through their self-righteous hypocrisy. He exposed their righteousness as being concerned more with external matters than with the inner matters of the heart—with mercy, love, and justice. But is Jesus only telling us that we should be as rigorous with the demands on our inner life as the Pharisees were with the externals? Or is he calling us beyond a merely quantitative extension of the righteousness of the Pharisees to a qualitatively different kind of righteousness—to a righteousness that belongs to a wholly new order because it belongs to the kingdom of heaven now come to earth in his person?

What essentially characterized the righteousness of the Pharisees is that it was their own. It belonged to each of them as an individual accomplishment or trait. As a personal possession, they could measure it, and they could compare themselves as having it with others who did not have it, or did not have it as fully as they did. Hence they could measure the righteousness of others by their own. They could set themselves up as the judge of others people's righteousness and, if need be, cast them out of the synagogue to preserve their own holiness. They could take pride in their own righteousness and display it before society. What characterized their righteousness, therefore, was that it set them apart from ordinary people, creating distance and divisiveness. Their very focus on righteousness as a possession of their own restricted their capacity to be responsive to others—to the man robbed and beaten on Jericho's road, to the publican in the temple, to the woman caught in adultery, and to Jesus himself. Their righteousness contributed to the brokenness of human life rather than serving to bring about reconciliation and a new wholeness among the people.

But bringing reconciliation and restoring wholeness is what the kingdom of heaven and its righteousness is all about. And that is the righteousness that Jesus embodied and preached as the good news of the kingdom of heaven. That is the righteousness that forms the framework for the Beatitudes with which Jesus began his ministry of proclamation.

The Beatitudes

The Beatitudes can be read and are often interpreted as if they call us to a righteousness very much like that of the Pharisees, to a piety that is our own, by which we can measure ourselves and

measure others. When thus interpreted, we hear Jesus identifying
eight desirable and important spiritual qualities which we should
be cultivating in ourselves and looking for in others if we and they
are to be found truly spiritual. Searching for these qualities, then,
found in some and not in others, will divide the sheep from the
goats, the true Christians from the nominal or false Christians.
What is more, we will insist that true happiness or blessedness
is to be found in our possessing these eight spiritual qualities: a
recognition of our neediness, a true sorrow for our sins, genuine
meekness, and a seeking after righteousness, as well as our being
merciful, pure in heart, peacemakers, and willing to endure
revilement for our righteousness. Sermons constantly admonish
us to examine whether we really do possess these spiritual qualities.

All of these are indeed admirable spiritual qualities. They are
also something of our own, possessions in ourselves as individuals
which we can measure and by which we can measure others.
There is nothing here that the Pharisees could not applaud and
also preach. Good and desirable as they are, they are not the
righteousness that belongs to the kingdom of heaven. The more we
focus on these qualities within ourselves, the more we will separate
ourselves from others. Unless our righteousness exceeds these
qualities, even at their best, we have not yet found the entrance to
the kingdom of heaven.

If we take another look at the Beatitudes, we can see in them
the good news that tells us how God does right, and sets things right
in a world gone wrong. As recorded in Matthew 5, the fourth and
the eighth beatitudes, "Blessed are those who hunger and thirst for
righteousness" (vs. 6) and "Blessed are those who are persecuted
for righteousness' sake" (vs. 10), each referring to righteousness,
suggest that the first four belong together as one unit, with the last
four forming a parallel unit.

The first four portray a world gone wrong. The poor in spirit
are those whose spirits are broken--from the wrong of others
and from their own wrongdoing. They have no hope left. Their
lives have lost all meaning; they mourn that loss and merely exist.
These meek ones have lost all power and dignity; the dominion
that belonged to them in the beginning as God's gift to his image-
bearers is in the hands of others. Like people dying for lack of
food, they are deprived of any semblance of righteousness or

justice. Here is a description of human responsiveness that has all but withered away. These are not conditions or qualities that are desirable for anyone. Happiness or blessedness is not found in these conditions.

Where, then, does their blessedness come from? How is it that the kingdom of heaven is theirs? Where is their comfort? By what right do these pitiful, impotent meek inherit the earth? How shall they ever be satisfied? And what has all this to do with "righteousness?"

To the hopelessly broken ones, God came in Jesus. He came to be with them, to embrace them in love, even while they were yet sinners and enemies (Rom. 5:8, 10). He came to validate the worth of their lives (cf. Matt. 6:26), to restore, to renew, and to make whole again. Their blessedness is found not in their own qualities but in God's presence among them and his love for them. He ate and drank with publicans and sinners, with cheating tax collectors and prostitutes. He also feasted just as often with hypocritical Pharisees. He stretched out his hand to outcast lepers and healed them. He gave sight to the blind, strength to the crippled and paralyzed, health to the demon-possessed, and even life to the dead. He gave acceptance to a woman of many husbands living with a man not her husband, and forgiveness to the woman caught in adultery. He fed the hungry crowds. He wept over their lack of responsiveness. Deliverance from the ills set forth in the first four Beatitudes at the outset of Jesus' ministry was accomplished for all the world when his righteousness saw completion in his sacrificial death, lifted up between earth and heaven: "and I, when I am lifted up from the earth, will draw all men to myself" (John 12:32).

The second set of four Beatitudes describes more directly the nature of Jesus' righteousness. He it is who is the merciful one, who pursues God's will to the end with purity of heart and singleness of mind. He is the peacemaker. It is he who is persecuted, crucified for righteousness' sake. Shuffled from high priest to Herod to Pilate, he was reviled, mocked, and beaten. Yet he did not seek his own right. From his cross he continued to be responsive: he acknowledged his own weakness in thirst, he cared for his mother, he gave acceptance to a dying thief, and he sought forgiveness for those who were crucifying him. Those who had exalted in their own individual right could not tolerate one who turns away from pursuing his own right, especially when he called on them to do the same; because he had called them to follow, not their own way, but the way that is right according to the kingdom of heaven, they had rejected him. And yet, in that very "kingdom of heaven" way of doing right, Jesus still embraced them from his cross with love and forgiveness. Forsaken and separated from the Father's bosom, he still claimed God as his God and committed his spirit into the Father's hands. He finished the Father's work of reconciliation.

Although the unifying theme of the Sermon on the Mount is righteousness, it has nothing to do with the righteousness of the Pharisees, the righteousness that can be called "our own." Instead, it has everything to do with the righteousness of the kingdom of heaven, with God's way of doing right, and with the righteousness of Jesus that covers or expiates our sin. Jesus' "righteousness" was not just an individual trait within himself by which he avoided all mistakes and moral lapses and kept the whole law to prove himself right and good as an individual. The death of such a one would not be inherently reconciling. Jesus' "food" was to do the Father's will, not to maintain his own right (John 4:34; cf. 5:19, 30; 6:38; cf. also Heb. 10:5-10). And the Father's will was to love the world, to reconcile the world to himself in Christ, and to save rather than to condemn the world (John 3:16-17). Jesus' righteousness is the manifestation of that purpose of God. Rather than being merely an individual trait, his righteousness inherently joined him to others, to sinners. He was not so much tempted to do evil as he was tempted to follow his own right, his individual good, but from that temptation he turned aside again and again (Luke 4:1-13). Unlike Eve and Adam in Eden's garden, he, in Gethsemane's garden, was able to say, "Not my will, but thine, be done" (Luke 22:42). That responsive righteousness of the kingdom of heaven is inherently reconciling because by it God in Christ embraces his enemies.

All the way to the end, Jesus was responsive to so much more than his own individual right. His responsiveness both to God and to those attending his crucifixion gives meaning and content to his sacrifice, to the reconciliation he came to achieve. Seeing God in Jesus dying for us on the cross gives us the assurance that we are indeed forgiven and reconciled. Reconciliation is not just a possibility; it is a "done deal" in Christ. The covenant relationship established in creation, but broken in the fall, is restored. The fractured circle of love between God and the world is healed. "God was in Christ reconciling the world to himself" (II Cor. 5:19). God's way of doing right, incarnate in Jesus of Nazareth, reconnects God with us in the cross of Christ.

It is Jesus' redeeming, reconciling righteousness, his way of doing right, his responsiveness both to God's will and to human need, that belongs to the kingdom of heaven come to earth. That is Jesus' way, God's way, of doing right--a righteousness that changes everything in a world gone wrong. The fruitless separation that occurred with the emergence of sin, that fateful separation which had no potential to enhance either us as human beings or our sovereign Creator-God, is overcome. We are given new names: "Redeemed," "Beloved," "Elect of God," and more. And God himself receives new names and a new identity: he is "Savior," "Redeemer," "Lord." And a new union, a new covenant relationship, is formed between the Redeemer and the Redeemed—a covenant of grace sealed by the blood of Jesus. His sacrifice represents the strange and wonderful new righteousness of the kingdom of heaven that embraces us sinners, his enemies, as his Beloved.

Paul identified this new "righteousness of God" (Rom. 1:17) as the power of the gospel. It cancels out the power of sin and shame. It places us under grace rather than under law (Rom. 6:14). It leaves us in the arms of a God who of his own will chooses to embrace us with his eternal love. In that embrace we *know* that everything is "all right" with us. Paul cannot but extol this new righteousness as "the free gift" (Rom. 5:16), as "the abundance of grace" (vs. 17), as "the free gift of righteousness" (vs. 17). And because reconciliation is found in the life of Christ, his resurrection and ascension enable us, centuries later, to live with him in this newness of life, in this new righteousness (cf. Heb. 7:23-25; Rom. 6:4).

But if it is all a free gift, if reconciliation simply reflects the "abundance of grace," and if the whole world is radically changed through Christ's righteousness by being reincorporated into the circle of God's love, what significance does our response of faith and hope and love have? Why not "sin so that grace may abound" (Rom. 6:1)? If it is all up to God's electing grace, where is our freedom? In the next chapter we reflect on the restoration of our responsivity.

5

RESPONSIVITY RESTORED

Reflections on Faith, Hope, and Love

The circle of trust–the covenant relationship–between the sovereign God and his responsive image-bearers is restored through "the free gift of righteousness" (Rom. 5:17). That righteousness is lived out in Christ Jesus to the very shedding of his blood on Calvary's cross.

In Jesus' sacrifice of himself on the cross for our sakes, it is as if he embraces God and God's will with one outstretched hand and embraces us sinners, his enemies, with the other outstretched hand. Thus he joins God and us together irrevocably from his cross. The circle of love between God and the world is once again made perfect. Because he lives and rules at the right hand of the Father, that once-broken but now-restored circle of love spans the ages–past, present, and forever.

And we are again free–free to respond as God in the beginning intended and created us to respond. But even more than that, we are free to respond as God in Jesus responded to us–out of the new righteousness that comes with the kingdom of heaven. As we look to what God has done in the past, in creation, in Israel, but above all in Christ, we are free to respond in *faith*. As we struggle with our own self-limiting fears and look to the uncertain future, we are free to respond with *hope*. Above all, as we live daily in all our complex relationships, we are free at last to live responsively in *love*, even toward an enemy!

Faith as Restored Responsivity

The essential character of Christian faith is that it is a response to something outside ourselves. By its own inner dynamic, faith embraces something or someone beyond itself. Otherwise faith becomes but another reenactment of the original sin, another way of making something in ourselves the measure of what is right or good. Christian faith is a human responsiveness that embraces the gifts of God's grace, whether from creation or from redemption. Redemption restores to us and enhances the responsivity that was lost by the fall into sin. Within the circle of God's redemptive love, hardened hearts become responsive again.

When Faith Functions as a Form of Circumcision

No issue stirred the passion of the apostle Paul more deeply than that of circumcision (cf. Romans 2:25 to 4:15; Galatians 1:6ff, 3:1ff, and 5:1-15; Philippians 3:2ff; Colossians 2:8-15). Paul saw the insistence on circumcision for Gentile believers and the keeping of other aspects of the Law of Moses as tantamount to a denial of Christ, a forsaking of the gospel, and a loss of essential Christian freedom. Circumcision has long ceased to be an issue in the Christian church, but could there be something in Paul's passion that continues to be of equal concern for us today? What was it about circumcision that concerned Paul so deeply? What characterized circumcision?

First, circumcision was a gift of God; it was "a sign or seal" (Rom. 4:11) of God's free gift of righteousness and forgiveness; its intent was to arouse a response of faith and trust in this gracious, all-providing God. Second, it became a permanent mark or possession in those who received it. Third, it came to distinguish those who possessed it from those who did not. And fourth, circumcision became a basis for separation from and judging of those who did not possess it.

Once Christ has come and established the newly responsive and reconciling righteousness of the kingdom of heaven, any insistence on circumcision as a separating and judging principle would deny the essential meaning of the gospel and its righteousness. It would destroy the essential meaning of Christ's coming and of the gospel as the good news of God's grace. Circumcision was given originally as a sign of God's grace, but circumcision after Christ's death would lead us to look at ourselves—at what we possess or are or have done—as being the measure of what is right and needed in the kingdom of God. As something in ourselves becomes the focus of our faith, faith loses its character as responsiveness to God's goodness, grace, and redemption.

Every gift of God's grace has the potential of being turned into and used as a form of circumcision. Even faith itself can and easily does begin to function in that way. Faith, which itself is a gift of God (Eph. 2:8), can be seen as a possession of our own which distinguishes those of us who have it from those who do not. The possession of faith then becomes the measure by which we judge others to be acceptable in the kingdom of heaven. It becomes a basis for separating ourselves from those who do not have what we have. Faith then functions like circumcision, denying the very grace it was intended to embrace.

The variety of ways in which faith can become a form of circumcision is endless. Faith can be turned into specific intellectual concepts which anyone who would enter the kingdom must agree to. We can then identify the "fundamentals," such as inerrancy of the Scriptures, the virgin birth, or the substitutionary atonement. These concepts become the object of our faith and the measure for judging true or born-again Christians and distinguishing them from others who are judged to be less-than-true Christians. In some circles, being "born again" appears to function as a form of circumcision. In others, it may be a matter of being "Reformed" or being "charismatic" or having some other identity. In other contexts it may be a matter of believing in some individual ethic or in some social moral code that functions as a possession of those who are "in" as distinguished from those who are "out."

None of us escapes the temptation to reenact the original sin by making something that we possess in ourselves the measure of what is right and good. Originally a response to the goodness, grace, and love of our sovereign God in creation and in redemption, our faith easily turns back on itself so that we make our believing something or other the "work," the "something right" that we do and others must also do to be acceptable. Then faith itself, like circumcision, inhibits our capacity to be responsive to others. Faith ceases to be simply the gift of God's grace that restores to us our responsivity toward God and toward all our fellow human beings.

Faith as Confession of Sin

Confession of sin belongs to the renewed responsiveness of faith. Confessing our sin, repenting, is not something we must first do before we will be received back into the circle of God's love. As Christ embraces us sinners with the righteousness that is from above, we are enabled to view ourselves and others in a wholly new light. Experiencing his embrace, we no longer need to be afraid of our sin. We can respond with courage by looking at the reality of who we are and what we do in making ourselves the measure of good and evil. We can look our manipulative ways of controlling others squarely in the eye; we can face our own pervasive tendency to blame and judge others as we justify ourselves; we can dare to recognize the pretenses behind which we hide ourselves from even those dearest to us. We can enter into confession because through faith we know that we are not under law but under grace. Sin has lost its fearsome power (Rom. 6:14).

The liturgy of the church's worship service traditionally has included a "Service of Reconciliation" which begins with a call to repentance and is followed by some form of confession of sin. This confession does not precede worship as a precondition, but is an integral part of worship. It comes after God's "Call to Worship" and after the "Greeting" that says it all: "Grace, mercy, and peace be to you from God our Father and our Lord Jesus Christ." Confession is simply one response that God's grace makes possible for us, a response that enlarges our capacity to renew relationships of love—with God and also with each other. For that reason confession need not be a dour moment, but can be one filled with an expectation of good things to come. We may even learn to deal with sin through a restored sense of humor.

Confession of sin is one of the forms the new responsiveness of faith takes. In sinning we make ourselves the measure of what is right and wrong; in confession of sin we give up that stance. We lose our fear; we lay aside our pretenses; we stop blaming and judging; we cease, at least for the moment, all manipulating for control. We stop focusing on what is wrong in others and what is right in ourselves. Everything that impedes our responsiveness to others and to God is laid aside in confession of sin. The possibilities of responding in new ways of loving and valuing each other are again opened up to us through confession of sin. We discover what

Jesus meant in the Sermon on the Mount (Matthew 5) when he repeatedly said, "You have heard that it was said…, but I say unto you…." In each case he is calling us to a confession that unites us with all other human beings instead of dividing us from them.

The doctrine of total depravity becomes a liberating expression of faith in this context. It is not a concept that needs to be defended as "right" against those who are wrong in rejecting it. Far less is it a pessimistic view of human life which implies that we may see little good in ourselves or in others. It is rather a confession of sin in which we are enabled to recognize and lay aside the divisive claims to our own righteousness. In confession we lay aside all of our own pretenses to being right or good in our individual selves in contrast to others. We are freed from our usual defensiveness about ourselves and therefore set free to experience and discover others in wholly new and unexpected ways.

Confession of sin, to be sure, can also become a new form of "circumcision." That occurs when we subtly begin to look at confession as a trait in ourselves that distinguishes and divides us from those who do not confess. What can prevent this arrogance? Only the keen sense that confession of sin is itself a form of the faith that looks away from ourselves to embrace the grace of God alone.

In the liturgical confession of sin in worship, we as Christians are not merely confessing our individual sins; we are confessing our solidarity with all human beings in sin. The church as the body of Christ is functioning as "a royal priesthood" (I Peter 2:9), bringing the sins of the world before the throne of grace. The liturgy of confession unites us with the rest of the world. Paradoxically, that is what distinguishes worshipping Christians from the rest of the world.

Faith as the Embracing of God's Grace

Faith involves the restoration of our responsivity, the renewal of our capacity to be responsive to all that our sovereign God has done and is doing. The very meaning of faith itself lies in our looking away from ourselves or anything in ourselves to a God whose grace, mercy, and peace are the source of "salvation" or wholeness and of never-ending growth in our relationship to him, to other human beings, and to all of creation.

The principle that was at work in God's creating the world is also at work in wondrously new ways in redemption. The more the sovereign God of grace works out his gracious will through his own way of doing right, the greater becomes the capacity of the creature to respond with freedom to God's working and to God's works. In Ephesians 3:14ff, Paul unfolds an expansive vision of the God who in Christ overcomes the division between Jew and Gentile in working reconciliation. Through a faith "rooted and grounded in love" we receive the power to comprehend the "breadth and length and height and depth" of God's love; we come "to know the love of Christ which surpasses knowledge," and we will ourselves "be filled with all the fullness of God." Faith in Christ restores our responsive capacities even beyond what they were in the beginning.

Faith, then, is not a condition for entering the kingdom of heaven. Faith is not at all something we must first show, as if it were a kind of admission ticket which we must possess in order for us to gain entrance into the kingdom and obtain the gift of salvation. Faith is rather the enjoyment of the kingdom of heaven. Faith is itself the salvation for which we long. To receive the gift of faith is to receive all of salvation. To receive salvation as a gift is to receive faith. Faith is the embracing of the "righteousness of God" by which God in Christ embraces us with his acceptance and love even while we as sinners are still his enemies. Faith represents a renewed capacity within us to be responsive to the grace of God in Christ, to acknowledge that there is nothing we possess that we have not received from him. For that reason faith cannot possibly be seen as a possession of our own that divides us from others. As Paul says to us, "For who sees anything different in you? What have you that you did not receive? If then you received it, why do you boast as if it were not a gift?" (I Corinthians 4:7). Faith responds to all of life, to all of redemption as to all of creation, by receiving it all as God's gift.

Faith as the Embracing of God's Election

Similarly, divine election is not some complicated notion impossible for ordinary people to understand. To the extent that it becomes that, it becomes virtually worthless–fascinating philosophical speculation at best, but still useless as far as faith is concerned. Faith by its very nature embraces a sovereign God who, out of his eternal love, himself chooses to love and redeem us in Christ. Faith looks to nothing found in the world or in ourselves for salvation, but only to a sovereign God who reveals in Christ his way of making things right (cf. Eph. 1:3ff). To talk about the righteousness of God revealed in Christ is to talk about an electing God, a God who chooses to make it right with us by embracing us with love in all our brokenness and lostness. Faith is a response to and a celebration of God's choosing, electing, to love us. Faith finds the source of our whole life and salvation as residing in the eternal being of God as a God of grace, mercy, peace, and love. The entire "doctrine of election" (or "predestination") is nothing more or less than the unfolding of the meaning of faith as a resting in "the righteousness of God" (Rom. 1:17) that is "the power of God for salvation" (Rom. 1:16).

A faith that rests in God's electing love can be as small as the tiniest mustard seed because faith is not concerned with its own size. The moment faith becomes concerned with itself and its own size, it is no longer a responsive faith, no longer a looking to and resting in the gracious God of creation and redemption. As our faith focuses instead on the fullness of God and what he has done, both in creation and in redemption, what we "take in" enhances us in our own responsiveness. We discover new meaning and hope in life, and we respond with renewed love to God, to his creation, and to all fellow image-bearers.

Hope as Restored Responsivity

A faith that looks back to what God's grace has accomplished turns into hope as we look forward to the future. "Those who mourn" (Matt. 5:4)–the broken, the powerless, those oppressed by injustice–have grounds for hope. "Theirs is the kingdom of heaven" (vs. 10); they will be comforted and will inherit the earth; "they shall be satisfied" (Matt. 5:6). Christian hope, grounded in faith, changes everything. Hope changes the way we look at the world and all its inhabitants. The world itself has a future. The earth–and the heavens, too–will become an inheritance.

Here, too, we are tempted to turn hope into another form of circumcision, a virtue or possession found in us that distinguishes and divides us from those who have no hope. Hope, seen as forward-looking faith, comes out of the renewed responsiveness that is ours because God in Christ has restored us to the circle of his love. Within that circle, in the renewed relationship of trust, we see God and his working in grace going before us into the future, and that casts its hue over all that we see as we look ahead and contemplate the future. Granted, the hue is a misty hue, perhaps like that found in many of Claude Monet's paintings; we see "in a mirror dimly;" we "know in part" (I Cor. 13:12). But what we see mistily, we see nonetheless with the varied colors of hope.

The Personalizing of Christian Hope

Hope relates to our individual lives in a personal way. Our jobs are never quite secure enough for us, our health is always precarious, our reputations are fragile, the fulfillment of our dreams and ambitions is always in question, and our relationships are never wholly stable. With anxiety having so much basis in reality, we can thank God that Christian hope is not a requirement that we must first meet in order to enter into the kingdom of heaven, for then none of us would enter.

Hope is a reality that each of us can embrace from within that kingdom, for the God of grace is the God of the future. The future we are invited to embrace with hope includes all of this life, but it does not end there. The salvation we embrace in faith today carries with it a hope that extends to all eternity. And the basis for that personal hope is the same as that for our faith—it is found in the grace of a God who is faithful even though we are faithless, whose lovingkindness and promises are forever sure, and whose own righteousness embraces us, sinners though we are. Christian hope is first of all a personal hope.

The Universalizing of Christian Hope

But Christian hope cannot remain merely individual. Our hope has no ground in ourselves nor in what we find in some other person. Hope cannot be grounded in our own or another's faith as one's possession. Christian hope is grounded in a faith that looks away from oneself to a gracious God. Because the faith out of which we live overcomes the individualism of original sin, it compels us to embrace others as we respond in hope.

So then to what extent do we dare to live out of that hope, grounded as it is in a faith that looks wholly to the grace of God? Suppose my daughter has rejected belief in God. Suppose my son is in wanton pursuit of the highs of crack cocaine. What if that son dies of an overdose? What if my daughter in a moment of desperation takes her own life? What if a loved one dies without naming the name of Jesus? And how do I live and work alongside my Jewish colleague, my Buddhist acquaintance, my humanist teacher, and the town atheist who zealously seeks to root out all traces of religion from public life? How shall I speak to and about those millions in the world who embrace other religions or no formal religion at all?

Speculative theological answers to questions such as these abound. The answers often take the form of some kind of judgment on those who do not have what we have. Theologians and churchmen have usually been unable to resist the temptation to give such answers. Conclusions for or against "universalism" can be justified as being reasonable deductions from what we see as the plain teaching of Scripture, and some of our deductive schemes can be truly ingenious. Yet such answers will only yield arguments about who and what is right versus who and what is wrong. The question of faith and the question of hope will not be addressed in such speculations. Whatever answer is given, our faith cannot possibly rest in that answer, for faith and hope rest in God alone, not in our circumscribed answers.

The real question is this: How can we live by faith and in hope as we face real-life situations? Because Christian faith is a response to the gifts of God's grace, Christian hope, rooted in that faith, also rests solely in the grace of God. Out of such hope, out of such a faith, we can live each day, responsive not just to God but to all our fellow human beings, however broken by sin. In Christian faith we confess that "all have sinned and fall short of the glory of God" (Rom. 3:23). Outside the circle of God's creative and redemptive love lie hopelessness and death. Human beings have devised many creative ways to God, but none of them, including our own, succeeds as "the way." That's a confession that binds us together in solidarity with all human beings, whatever their lot or status in life. Whenever we set ourselves up as the measure of what is right and good, we separate ourselves from the source of all goodness and grace. Then what I do religiously from out of my self will not bring me or anyone else hope and salvation. That is something I know about myself just as well as about any wayward daughter, son, co-worker, or neighbor.

But, praise God! The hope I have for myself is a hope I can have for anyone, even for a wayward child, an unbeliever, a Buddhist, or the town atheist! The hope I can have for them is not that they will eventually come to do "the right thing," but that God is a gracious God and that he comes with a righteousness that is his own—and not my child's, the Buddhist's, or the atheist's. God's, and not theirs. God's, and not mine. Like the confession of sin, so also the confession of grace becomes the basis for a hope that unites me in solidarity with all people everywhere. That is a hope by which I can live even in the most troubled of relationships, because a hope grounded in the grace of God transforms *me* in my vision of and relationship to the other.

A woman in her mid-thirties asked me recently whether there was any hope for her father's eternal salvation. The father had sadistically abused her and an older sister sexually as children. He now denies everything and refuses to have any contact with the daughters unless and until they also deny that it ever happened. I can hardly think of a situation with less hope than this one. If hope is grounded in human decisions or qualities, there is no hope possible for such a father.

We reflected together on the hope that she has for herself, and I for myself. We agreed that, in regard to ourselves, we rested in the grace of God as the basis for our personal hope. Why, then, could she not live with the very same hope for her abusive father? "But what if he dies without repenting?" she asked. A good question. She wanted an answer. We always want to "know," to be sure that we are "right." We want to be able to judge. A part of her still wants to know that her father will burn in hell forever for what he did to her and her sister, as he deserves. Yet another part of her really does want to believe that there is hope for her father. The tension within her will not quickly go away or be easily resolved. But as her faith refocuses again and again on God's grace she will live with growing hope. And that hope will gradually contribute to her own healing, to a slow renewing of her own capacity to respond to life with joy and peace and love. Such hope, like the faith out of which it springs, is limitless. And hope, as the restoration of our responsivity, gives rise to limitless possibilities of love.

Love as Restored Responsivity

Faith looks back into the past to what God's grace has accomplished in Christ; faith looks forward to the future with an expansive hope in all of our relationships. Hope built on such a faith rediscovers the possibilities of love each day of our lives. "*So faith, hope, love abide, these three; but the greatest of these is love*" (I Cor. 13:13).

Why is love greater than hope, and greater than even faith itself? Just as hope springs from all that is present in faith while adding a new future-directed dimension to faith, so, too, love springs from all that is present in faith and hope. Love brings the renewed responsiveness of faith and hope to fruition in present relationships. Love is the completion of faith and hope. Without love, faith and hope are useless, as Paul indicates at the beginning of I Corinthians 13: "If I speak in the tongues of men and of angels, but have not love, I am a noisy gong or a clanging cymbal. And if I have prophetic powers, and understand all mysteries and all knowledge, and if I have all faith, so as to remove mountains, but have not love, I am nothing. If I give away all I have, and if I deliver my body to be burned, but have not love, I gain nothing." With the emergence of love, faith and hope finally achieve their intended purpose in our lives. In love the restoration of our responsivity is completed. The circle of trust is made whole through love.

Like faith and hope, love finds its source and power in God. Our love is our renewed responsiveness to God's love that was poured out first in creation, then on Israel, and finally on his beloved Son, the Christ—and through him on the whole world. "We love because he first loved us" (I John 4:19). Because his redemptive love toward us restores to us the capacity to respond in love, it really does become possible for us to respond to other human beings in love.

Love is our capacity to respond to the being of another person with respect, with the anticipation and desire that we will contribute to his or her development, growth, or well-being as a person. Love also includes our openness to learning and growing from our interactions with the person loved. With our responsivity restored through faith, we are empowered to grow with each interaction. Love overcomes the obstacles that impede our capacity to be responsive to the other.

Love: The Power that Overcomes Fear

Earlier (chapter 3) we noted that fear is the first human emotion that is directly identified and personally owned in the biblical narratives: "I was afraid, because I was naked; and I hid myself" (Gen. 3:10). The moment I make myself the measure of good and evil, I become vulnerable (naked). I can now be hurt by others who see not me but themselves as the measure of right and wrong, and I will probably not measure up. They also can now be hurt by me. Fear dominates human life. Fear destroys and replaces trust. Fear leads to the escalation of innumerable power struggles, and limits our capacity to be responsive to each other, to listen to each other, to understand each other, and to care about each other.

Significantly, the New Testament begins by acknowledging the dominance of fear in human life. When the angel Gabriel appears to Zechariah in the temple to announce that his wife Elizabeth will become pregnant with the forerunner of the Messiah, the first words that Gabriel speaks to him are, "Do not be afraid, Zechariah..." (Luke 1:13). Six months later the angel Gabriel appears to a virgin, Mary of Galilee, and says, "Do not be afraid, Mary" (Luke 1:30). An angel then appears in a dream to Joseph and says, "Joseph, son of David, do not fear..." (Matt. 1:20). When the Christ-child was born in Bethlehem, an angel full of glory appeared to shepherds at night, and the first words spoken were, "Be not afraid" (Luke 2:10). Jesus addressed the same fear in the Sermon on the Mount when he said, "Therefore I tell you, do not be anxious about your life..." (Matt. 6:25). And when Mary Magdalene and the other Mary approached Jesus' tomb after his burial, they were met by an angel whose first words were, "Do not be afraid" (Matt. 28:5).

It's not that God, or Jesus, condemns us for our fears. It is rather that in coming to us he addresses us where we live—in the reality of our fear-filled lives. He calls us out of our brokenness into the peace of his own presence. The apostle John sensed this purpose of Jesus' coming when he wrote, "There is no fear in love, but perfect love casts out fear" (I John 4:18). As we experience—or simply trust—God's perfect love toward us, our capacity to respond to God and to others in love is enlarged as our fears dissipate.

Love casts out fear because in love we need no longer make ourselves the measure of what is good or right. In love I become responsive to the other's need or well-being. I can risk being vulnerable. I can share myself with another. In love I no longer need to blame or stand in judgment on the other, or deal with issues of conflict by controlling, manipulating, or trying to change the other. Even the enemy, one who wishes me ill or who seeks to destroy me or has already done great harm, can be seen as a person toward whom I have some capacity to respond in love. All those aspects of human life in which fear impedes our responsiveness to each other and to God are renewed in freedom when we are embraced within the circle of love and trust that overcomes fear.

Faith that produces hope embraces all persons, however different from ourselves, as one with us in dependence on God's goodness and grace. The renewal that comes with faith and hope is completed as our responsive capacity is so enlarged as to embrace all persons in love.

Love vs. the Sin Against the Holy Spirit

But what happens when we lay claim to faith, and even to hope, but are without the spirit of love? In Matthew 12, having promised that every sin and blasphemy will be forgiven men, Jesus goes on to refer to "the blasphemy against the Spirit" which will not be forgiven (vs. 31). Is Jesus here making an exception to the assurance that every sin will be forgiven? If so, can we ever be certain that we have not committed this one exceptional and somewhat mysterious sin? Can we then ever really be sure of God's total forgiveness?

It seems to me that Jesus is not giving an exception here at all, but is rather referring to sin on a wholly different level from that of our actions. Nor is Jesus referring to something that cannot be identified until the end of life or the final judgment—a notion that for all practical purposes would render this word of Jesus quite useless. Jesus is referring to something that he experienced repeatedly and that we encounter just as often—in others and perhaps in ourselves as well.

As Matthew describes it, Jesus had passed through the grain fields with his disciples on the Sabbath. Being hungry, the disciples plucked the heads of grain to quiet their hunger pangs. Pharisees, unconcerned about their discomfort, seized on the event to criticize the disciples and Jesus. Jesus patiently explained to them the purpose of the law as being to preserve and enhance human life. Entering the temple, Jesus saw a man with a withered hand, and when they asked, "Is it lawful to heal on the Sabbath?" (Matt. 12:10) Jesus again explained the purpose of Sabbath laws, and then healed the man's hand. Instead of responding with joy at this man's healing, the Pharisees went out and plotted how they could destroy Jesus.

At this point we read that Jesus, aware of their plotting, withdrew from there. The implication is that further explanations were futile. Jesus had no interest in deliberately provoking the Pharisees. While he continued his healings, he instructed those he healed to tell no one; testimonies no longer served a purpose. But when a blind and mute demoniac was healed and could not keep silent, word got back to the Pharisees. Once again, instead of rejoicing with the healed demoniac, they now accused Jesus of being in league with the devil himself.

In this context Jesus distinguished sin against the Son of Man, which will be forgiven, from sin against the Holy Spirit, which will not be forgiven. The implication is that the Pharisees have been sinning not just against Jesus but against the Spirit. What was their "unforgivable sin?"

The Pharisees had spoken ill of Jesus' disciples and of Jesus himself. That sin will be forgiven. They had treated the man with the withered hand as a nobody, and went on to plot to destroy Jesus. All of that will be forgiven. They did the same to the healed demoniac, and again falsely accused Jesus, but that, too, will be forgiven. Even the later act of crucifying the Son of God was forgivable, as Jesus himself demonstrated from his cross. Nothing that the Pharisees did, no sin that they actually committed or could conceivably commit, was too heinous to be forgiven. We can take comfort that the same applies to any imaginable act of sin that we might commit. It will be forgiven—that is Jesus promise to us. There is *no exception.*

What, then, is unforgivable? Beneath the acts of sin portrayed in this chapter lies a deeper dimension of sin. The Pharisees betrayed a *spirit* within them that increasingly revealed itself as being incapable of responding in love. They could not see the disciples' hunger; they saw only a rule broken. They could not see the pain, emotional and physical, in the man with a withered hand; they only saw an opportunity to entrap Jesus. They could not see the love of God in Jesus' healings; the more he healed, the more they hated him and conspired to kill him. All of their acts of sin will be forgiven—without exception. But more is at work here, Jesus is saying. Forgiveness may be endless, but endless forgiveness will change nothing here. Something more is needed than forgiveness. Here is sin of spirit against Spirit. What is needed is not forgiveness alone; what is needed is a new spirit created within.

David sensed this deeper need in himself when he came to confess his sin concerning Bathsheba. In Psalm 51 he prays first for mercy, but then he prays, "Create in me a clean heart, O God, and put a new and right spirit within me" (vs. 10). David needed more than forgiveness; he needed a new spirit. The Pharisees needed more than forgiveness; they, too, needed a new and right spirit. And so do I; so do we all. We need the new spirit of love that comes from God's love, which was present and demonstrated in the life and healings of Jesus.

How restricted these Pharisees were in their capacity to be responsive in love to persons in need! The sin against the Spirit bespeaks a loss of that capacity. The spirit of love is a gift of God, not an achievement of ours. Hence it is not our role to judge the Pharisees, but rather to pray for the gift and spirit of love within ourselves so that we may be increasingly responsive to others in need—responsive in love, indeed, toward all God's creatures, including "pharisees" of our time whose spirit sins against the Spirit of love.

Love: The Supreme Expression of Freedom

With the advent of sin, a new expression of freedom came into being—a form of freedom that we have been living with ever since, but not really enjoying. It is the freedom to do our own thing, to seek our own good as measured by individual desires or needs alone, without genuine regard for others. It is the freedom to act in relationships without love. It is the freedom to act in a way that undermines trust. This is a freedom that destroys relationships and prevents individual growth. It is a freedom that leads to death of the spirit.

The original freedom that we lost through the fall into sin, however, is available to us today as fully as it was before the fall. In the beginning our freedom lay in our responsiveness to a God of overflowing love and goodness. His sovereign grace empowered us to be responsive not only to him but to all his creation, to all the creatures of his world, and to all who bear God's image. In that responsive love and trust we could be naked and not ashamed in each other's presence, even as male and female. The sovereignty of his all-powerful grace did not limit but created and expanded our freedom to live and love and grow.

In the fall, as trust was broken, this freedom was lost. But in Jesus, crucified and risen for us, this freedom—the freedom to love—is restored and available to us again.

Paul sees this freedom as the essence of the gospel. We are tempted to limit Christian freedom or liberty to those areas of life that are "adiaphora," that belong to the non-essential things of Christian faith and life. Not so for Paul. In Galatians 5:1 he writes, "For freedom Christ has set us free." Every essential truth of the gospel is contained in this freedom. Why did Christ enter our world? "For freedom!" exclaims Paul. What was the nature of his work while here? "Christ has set us free!" exclaims Paul. So who is this Christ as a person? He is the Liberator! Paul's concern is not that we may claim too much freedom. His deep concern is that we will lose the freedom that Christ has given us and will become enslaved again (vs. 2).

How do we lose our freedom? For Paul, freedom is lost through "circumcision" (Galatians 5:3-12), through the works of the flesh or the law—that is, our own works. When our own works again become the focus of our concern, we have "fallen away from grace" (vs. 4). The moment we claim that our loving is the "something right" that we do, we turn it into a form of "circumcision" by which we distinguish and divide ourselves from others who do not love as we do, and that, in turn, diminishes our capacity to love. The freedom to love then loses its character as a response to grace. It ceases to be the freedom for which we were created and redeemed–the freedom to love others as God has graciously loved us. Focus on our own works stands in contrast to "the hope of righteousness" for which we wait "through the Spirit" (vs. 5).

In Jesus Christ the freedom to love is as fully available to us today as it was in the beginning. The freedom to love unites us together with Christ in pursuit of the righteousness of the kingdom, expressed in the second set of beatitudes (Matt. 5:7-10). We become free with Christ to pursue with single-mindedness the business of mercy and peacemaking, even in the face of opposition (Matt. 5:11). This freedom is ours not as an accomplishment to be achieved by our independent efforts, but as a gift.

So we discover in redemption, as we did in the original creation, that the working of God's sovereign grace does not in any way impede or limit our freedom. On the contrary, the working of his sovereign will through grace enhances our freedom to be image-bearers of God who exercise our responsive capacity to love, and hence to grow and develop without limits, through all of life–now and through all eternity.

Servanthood: The Embodiment of Faith, Hope, and Love

When faith, hope, and love are present together, the "whole" formed in us is the self-emptying "mind of Christ" set forth in Philippians 2:5ff. Although he was God himself, Christ did not cling to divine prerogatives of glory and power. He took on the form of a servant and became obedient even to death on a cross. Subject to God, he served others–to lift them up, to exalt "those of low degree" as Mother Mary sang in her Magnificat (Luke 1:52). The model of servanthood which Jesus commended to his disciples (see Matt. 18:1-5, Mark 9:33-37; 10:42-45; Luke 9:46ff) and which he himself embodied in the washing of their feet (John 3:12-17) is the same as that found in the call to freedom which we examined in Galatians 5:13: "Through love be servants of one another." The model of servanthood here put forth is not that of weak passivity as embodied in the "doormat" personality, for that life-style comes from fear. This servanthood proceeds from the strong responsivity of restored faith, hope, and love. Little wonder, then, that this "mind of Christ" becomes the model for all relationships that the New Testament writers describe.

Servanthood: The Pervasive Model

The manner in which Paul draws on the "mind of Christ," the servant model, is illuminating. It is not merely that he calls all Christians to follow the example of Christ. He specifically addresses relationships which have been unequal in power throughout human history, and he applies to them the model of servanthood. He deals with rulers and subjects (Romans 13), with husbands and wives (Eph. 5:21-33), with parents and children (Eph. 6:1-3), and with masters and slaves (Eph. 6:5-9). In each of these pairings the first-mentioned traditionally has the power, and the second is without power, is weak in relation to the first. In each case Paul first addresses the weaker, the powerless ones in the relationship, and calls them to submission or servanthood. He calls on subjects to submit to the ruling authorities; he commends subjection of wives to their husbands, calls on children to obey their parents, and instructs slaves to submit to their masters. In each case this submission is related to a deeper submission that belongs to the Lord. Grasping for power is not the way to renew relationships. Such grasping limits the capacity to be responsive to the other.

Now if that were all that Paul said he could be seen as the great champion of the status quo, favoring those who already are in power and keeping those who are powerless in their place. But Paul has two more things to say.

First, he makes it clear that those in the traditional positions of power are equally subject to the Lord. Rulers have no power or authority except what God gives them; reverence for Christ is to govern husbands as well as wives; the Lord's instruction is what must govern the parents' raising of their children; and slaveowners are reminded that they and their slaves have the same Master in heaven. Hence, the powerful and the powerless have one thing in common: they are both subject to the Lord. All are called to live out of their faith in God.

Second, Paul consistently redefines the power position as a servant role in relation to the weaker party. The ruling authorities are to be servants who seek the good of their subjects. Husbands are to be like Christ in giving themselves up for the betterment of their wives. Parents (fathers in particular) are not to exasperate their children but are to bring them *up*. And as slaves are called to serve "with a good will as to the Lord" (Eph. 6:7), masters are called to "do the same to them, and forbear threatening" (vs. 9).

Both sides in these relationships are called on to give up the grasping for or clinging to power. Both sides are to see themselves as servants of God. Both sides are called to be servants to each other. All of this belongs to "the mind of Christ" (I Cor. 2:16). The resulting relationships of mutual servanthood are grounded in faith, and relationships grounded in faith are full of hope and of new possibilities for the future. The responsivity of each side toward the other is renewed by the transforming "mind of Christ" (cf. Rom. 12:1-2).

Servanthood: The Key to Hermeneutics

The doctrine of Scripture, including the principles of hermeneutics, is often treated in systematic theology as a "prolegomenon," that is, as something that must be determined before we discover what the Scriptures actually say to us. There may be some advantages to systematizing theology in that way. There is also considerable danger in doing so.

The danger is that we will formulate a "doctrine" of Scripture which then functions as a new form of "circumcision." What we are told we must believe beforehand about the Scriptures will be separated from the message that God addresses to us in his word. The responsiveness which the word of God rekindles and enlivens within us will be reduced to theoretical formulas about the Scriptures which we must believe, lest we be judged to have a low and unfaithful view of Scripture. The crucial questions then will be whether we adhere to the "right" view of verbal inspiration and inerrancy or infallibility. Holding to the right formula becomes the "something right" that we must do to be acceptable, in contrast to those who hold the "wrong" view. How easily we reenact the original sin in our theologizing! And, like the advocates of circumcision in Paul's day, in the name of holding on to the faith of old we effectively deny the grace of God by clinging to our own righteousness, bringing divisiveness and destroying relationships.

How can we avoid dealing with the Scriptures in a legalistic way? Legalism leads us to treat the Bible as if it were a source book from which we are to derive numerous instructions for individual life, for life in the church, and for belief, all of which we must then observe. Once we have done so, these tenets become our own possession; they become the basis for measuring and judging the faith of others. Then our very beliefs about the Scriptures function as a form of our own righteousness that divides us from others, and becomes "another gospel" that undermines the grace of God.

What if, instead, we reflect back on hermeneutics from out of and as a part of our renewed responsiveness to God and his work of grace? Then hermeneutics becomes a postscript rather than a prolegomenon. Then, in looking back, we discover that Scripture is the very word that has elicited and awakened the new responsiveness within us toward God and all his creatures. We discover that these are the words that have awakened within us a new sense of the sovereign grace that sets us free to trust and to hope and to love.

What are we doing, then, when we respond in the "right" way—that is, in faith—to the Scriptures as God's word? We are trusting God's graciousness toward us and others, and, because of that, we have hope for all those whom we meet. And we can therefore respond to them in love, as servants. Only in so doing are we embracing the Scriptures as God's own word to us.

The primary principle of hermeneutics, therefore, can be seen as the principle of servanthood. Becoming a servant is the same as having a new responsiveness. From beginning to end, we read and listen to the word of the Scriptures to hear what they have to say about our being and becoming servants—servants to the sovereign God of grace, mercy, and peace, and therefore servants to each other and to all people. In this way we come to recognize that our responsiveness to the Scriptures and our new responsiveness to God and to each other are one and the same.

This renewal of faith, hope, and love in and among us overcomes the fruitless and destructive separations that occurred in the fall. Out of the renewed responsiveness of faith we are empowered to build relationships of love that are filled with hope.

How can our renewed freedom for responsive living in love come to expression in our lives as individuals, as married couples, as family members, as the church, and as members of society? That will be the theme we develop throughout Part II.

LIVING RESPONSIVELY

Part II

RESPONSIVE LIVING
in a
REDEEMED WORLD

6

LIVING RESPONSIVELY
as an **INDIVIDUAL**

Each of us as a human being is an individual who lives within a network of relationships. As such we each experience some kind of polarity between our individuality and our commitment to our various relationships, which sets up a tension which can be either immobilizing or creative.

Does entering into a relationship require the suppression of individuality? I can assert my individuality in a way that risks the breakdown of a significant relationship, or I can set aside my personal needs, desires, or interests in order to hold on to a relationship. What takes priority, my personal growth, or cultivation of my relationships? Is it possible to promote both at the same time?

We can live creatively with this tension when we recognize that *responsivity belongs to the core of our individuality*. Our individuality best comes to expression in those uniquely human ways in which we are responsive to the world and to other persons in the world. In fact, this process works both ways. The more my individual capacity for responding grows, the more I am able to form significant relationships of intimacy. And the cultivation of broader and deeper relationships is precisely what expands my responsive capacity and thus promotes my individual growth. Wherever we experience these two working together we discover glimpses of grace in a world already redeemed, though still broken.

So let's explore various dimensions of our individuality from the viewpoint of our capacity to be responsive as individuals. In succeeding chapters we can then explore the interplay between our individuality and various forms of relationships that are important to us as human beings and as Christians living in a redeemed world.

Facing our Finitude

As individuals we have an infinite potential for human development and growth. That sounds wonderful and expansive! But somehow we keep bumping up against the reality of our own finitude, the reality of our limitations and our fears. We are not, after all, God. We are not all-knowing or almighty or infinite. We can only be in one place at a time. Growing or not, we will remain limited in all our human capacities.

The Extent and Limits of Growth

Everything that makes me the individual that I am will contribute to my capacity to be responsive. But at the same time, all the diverse parts of me will also mark the boundaries of my responsive capabilities. My physiology, my personality, my sexuality, the developmental history that I experienced within my family of origin—all will contribute both to the extent and to the limits of my responsive capabilities.

The physiology that I have inherited will affect my capacity for responding to life's physical challenges. My stature, strength, agility, and overall health will both enable and limit my ability to engage in athletics, my willingness to engage in physical activities, and even my capacity to participate in certain forms of artistic expression. The strength and quality of my vocal cords, for example, will influence my singing ability. Chemical and other physiological processes in the chromosomes and in my brain will affect both my emotional and my intellectual responsively. Everything that belongs to my physiology will both enable my self expression and will determine my limits.

My personality, largely genetically determined, enables me to express myself and respond to all of life as the person I am. But the personality that is mine will keep me from reacting to situations in the same way that you do. And this factor, too, will influence the extent and the limits of my intellectual, emotional, aesthetic, moral, and spiritual development and pursuits.

My sexuality enables me to express myself responsively but also sets limits to what I can do. As a male, I can do what no female can do, but I cannot bear children. A woman can do what no male can do, but she cannot grow a beard or sire offspring. Each person's whole experience of life will be conditioned by masculinity or femininity, both mentally and emotionally. Sexuality both colors and limits the way you and I each respond to life, as well as the way we respond to God and to his word.

How I deal with all of these inherited aspects of my individuality will be molded by my experiences in the family in which I grew up. I may have learned to celebrate my strengths and accept my limits. Or I may have come to distrust my worth and to fear that my inadequacies will make me unacceptable. The giving or withholding of approval and acceptance in a family so profoundly shapes a child's sense of self that its impact commonly lasts a lifetime. The same is true of how feelings like hurt and anger are allowed expression, and of how control and dominance are experienced and conflicts managed. Equally important is the room given for the conveying of love and warmth, for the communication of respect for privacy and differences of opinion, and for the teaching of moral, religious, aesthetic, and intellectual values. All of these factors together provide a reservoir of experience on which the adult that I now am will draw all my life. But all of these also provide limits to my capacity to respond in the various relationships and experiences of my adult life.

Any experience of abuse in childhood and adolescence, whether emotional, physical, or sexual in nature, limits one's capacity to respond. The more persistently trust has been broken, the more persistently fear takes control. Healing and personal growth always involve reworking the meaning of old hurts and working through those emotional blocks that still impede one's growth. In varying degrees we all have some of these issues to deal with in our lives.

Individuals who are struggling with severe emotional pain that blocks their personal growth are often impatient to get on with and complete their recovery. Who can blame them? The answer is that they themselves can. They blame themselves particularly when problems that once seemed resolved or "worked through" seem to recur. Such persons often are hard on themselves for being

30, 40, or 50 years old and still (or again) having to deal with the same old problems of anxiety and depression, or with old feelings of inadequacy or insignificance or worthlessness, or with old compulsions which were present years before. Telling themselves repeatedly that they should have worked these through by now reinforces all the old processes that blocked their continuing development in the first place. Old fears die hard! In fact, they often reemerge at a new stage in life to block our growth in responsivity. Growing beyond the pain never occurs quickly enough, and then a self-imposed standard for progress reinforces the old negative feelings and becomes self-defeating.

In the Light of Eternity

A perspective from eternity can be helpful. Think of yourself as having an eternity in which to live and grow through all your interactions with the vast created universe, with all those who share eternity with you, and with our infinite God. You have an infinite capacity to keep on growing. Each facet of the universe that you encounter and each person with whom you interact will contribute something toward expanding your capacity to respond more fully than before. You grow through your here-and-now experience of another person, as does your friend through hers of you. The two of you meet again, say, 10,000 years later, after each of you has experienced much more of creation, of other human beings, and of God. At that point she will have become a more fully developed human being. And so will you. Thus you will each have a new capacity to stimulate further growth in the other. And so it will be among all who are there, and with all facets of an ever-changing physical universe with which we interact, and with God himself. Though we will always remain finite, the possibilities for further growth are endless through all eternity. Each person will develop his and her own unique possibilities, with no two of us alike. That, to me, is a far more fascinating fantasy for eternity than one of standing around forever singing hymns!

And far more useful. It puts things in perspective for us here and now. A perspective from eternity can help us lay aside our fears that we are not growing fast enough or progressing far enough in our journey of 30, 45, or 60 years thus far. It takes our growth or progress out of the arena of an accomplishment that we must "succeed at" or "measure up to" if we are to feel acceptable. We can give ourselves permission to get on with the business of living and growing, each in our own way and at our own pace, enjoying whatever new responses we are able to develop. Measuring up is out of the picture! We will never "arrive," thank God! We will always have new gifts to open up in the unfolding of our individuality. Thus we begin to discover in a practical way what it means to live in a redeemed world where we are "under grace" and not "under law."

One intriguing paradox in human growth is that the more we accept the varying limitations derived from our finitude and from our self-limiting fears, the more we are enabled to grow beyond them. Our tendency, though, is to cling to a fear of our limitations and thus limit rather than promote the growth of our responsive capabilities; this fear then ends up impeding our growth far more that the limitations themselves.

Living Defensively

Out of fear, most of us as individuals tend to live much of our lives either defensively or aggressively, or with some combination of each. I live defensively when I withdraw from others or from life's opportunities out of my fear of being hurt. I am protecting myself from a form of pain that I do not want. Some examples: An adolescent boy wants badly to ask an attractive girl to go with him on a date, but he puts off calling her until it is too late; avoiding asking her protects him from the feared pain of rejection that he could experience should she turn him down. A student in a classroom holds back her ideas regarding a question the teacher has asked; she fears that her ideas will sound naïve or stupid to the others, and doesn't want to be laughed at; by remaining quiet she protects herself from that humiliation. A young man opposed to a current war finds himself in a group of people who are expressing patriotic support for the government's conduct of the war; by keeping quiet he protects himself from being labeled unpatriotic or, worse, a coward. An employee is insulted by her boss, but she restrains her anger lest her boss think ill of her, thus protecting herself from the feared pain of being rebuked or even fired. You would like to have more friends, but make few efforts to reach out, worried that no one would really want to be your friend anyway, afraid to face the pain that a rejected overture of friendship could cause.

In each case, the response is a defensive one. The aim is to protect ourselves from some feared consequence or hurt. In itself there is nothing wrong with responding defensively. We all have the right to protect ourselves from too much pain. There is even wisdom in doing so at times. We need the protection of our fig leaves.

Living defensively becomes a problem only when the main pattern of our response to life is a defensive one. Such a pattern becomes self-restrictive and inhibits the growth in a person's responsiveness and individuality. It also limits the development of healthy relationships. The more pervasive the defensive pattern is, the less successfully it will work as a means of protection from further pain. It becomes a self-defeating pattern, because in the long run it brings a greater pain derived from constantly experiencing a fearful and restricted life-style. As a rule, the more an individual has experienced hurt or abuse of any kind–in childhood, but also later in life–the more limited and defensive will be his or her responses to life as an adult.

Living Aggressively

I live aggressively whenever I am intent on imposing my own ideas, attitudes, feelings, needs or actions on others without regard for who they are and without respect for their ideas, feelings, and needs. I mask my fear of intimacy when I live aggressively. The adolescent boy who responds aggressively will not fear rejection in asking a girl for a date, but will be ready to ridicule any girl who would dare to turn him down. In the classroom, the aggressive person will assert her opinion as if it were the only one that had any validity to it, and will discount any ideas that conflict with her own. Let the boss insult the bold employee who is expressing anger and she may swear at him on the spot and demand an instant apology.

In contrast to the withdrawal and avoidance that characterize the responses of the person who lives defensively, the person who lives aggressively can be characterized as one who is quick to go on the attack, at least verbally, and sometimes physically as well. Wife-beaters in the home and despots among nations respond to life aggressively. But so do those who are quick to blame others whenever something goes wrong, resorting to name-calling when angry, and caricaturing the other party. Operating from a position of power, they attempt to manipulate and intimidate others by the force of their opinion or anger, or even by their hurt. Such persons either feel no need for compliments from others, or else demand them because they feel entitled to the admiration of others. If persons who respond defensively to life tend to trust and accept *their own* responses too little, those who respond aggressively tend to trust and value the responses of *others* too little. The former tend to pull away from others, while the latter tend to push others away from them.

Again, the ability to respond aggressively is not in itself bad. Insofar as it displays a healthy confidence in oneself and the ability to be assertive, this way of dealing with life has its benefits. Such persons at least let others know where they stand, and they often accomplish many worthwhile goals. The problem with getting stuck in this way of responding is that it turns out to be self-limiting. It is a way of responding that limits one's opportunities to get to know other persons intimately, thus depriving oneself of the benefits of learning from others and of expanding one's own capacity to grow.

Responding aggressively also restricts our capacity to get to know ourselves. The more I insist that I am always right and others wrong, and the more I verbally or physically attack those who disagree with me or cross me, the less I will be able to reflect on and understand my own feelings and actions. In this way, too, my own growth is stymied. Living aggressively, like living defensively, restricts our capacity to develop our own individuality. And flipping back and forth between responding defensively and reacting aggressively merely adds variety, not growth, to our lives.

Growth through Living Responsively

To be human is to live responsively. It is not the case that most people fail to live responsively and need to be taught to do so. No one needs a "how-to-do-it" book on living responsively, any more than we need instruction on how to breathe. To live and breathe as a human being is to live responsively.

What we do need, however, is to acknowledge and recognize that we live in a redeemed world; we are free to affirm life as fully as we can, free to develop those facets of life that will enhance rather than diminish our individual responsive capacities.

The Affirmation of Individual Responsibility

All issues in personal growth, like all problems in human relationships, involve sorting out "who is responsible for what." In referring to responsibility here, I do not mean primarily blame or even duty, though these may be involved; responsibility as *accountability* is more the issue here. We acquire a growing sense of our individuality, and function best in relationships, when we are willing to acknowledge that the responses which come out of us are an expression of who we are. We are accountable for them.

We often do the opposite. Often we treat ourselves as if we were responsible for what someone else does. We take on ourselves a responsibility that really does not belong to us but belongs to another; at the same time we lay on someone else the accountability for what is really our own doing. Another person speaks (or, we may suspect, just *thinks*) ill of us, and we automatically ask ourselves what we have done wrong, assuming that we are responsible for what the other says or even thinks. We do the same when others get angry with us—we make ourselves the issue rather than letting the other be accountable for whatever he or she is saying or thinking or feeling.

Having made ourselves responsible for what someone else does (says, thinks, feels), we are then likely to react either defensively or aggressively. Our feelings will be "hurt." We may become angry and attack back, blaming the other person for how we respond. We make another person responsible for what are *our own* feelings and reactions, while denying responsibility for what *is* our doing and making ourselves feel responsible for what *is not* ours. Chances are the other party is doing much the same. No wonder conflicts often escalate out of control!

We affirm our individuality when we take full responsibility for our own actions, words, thoughts, and feelings while allowing others to be responsible for theirs. The more we affirm all aspects of our individual selves and claim them as our own responsibility, the more growth we will experience in our personal lives.

The Affirmation of Feelings

Growth in our individuality involves affirming our own feelings as an integral part of who we are as persons. My own feelings represent my uniquely individual capacity to respond with some form of inner intensity to the created world as I experience it, to other persons who impact my life, and even to God himself. My feelings are the internal register of the significance I give to external events–to those circumstances and/or actions of others that impinge on my life. My feelings are a part of my created capacity to respond to life and to all of reality outside myself.

There are several ways of dealing with our own feelings that will constrict rather than enhance our capacity to be responsive emotionally. They are all variations on the theme of devaluing our own feelings. We devalue our feelings when we look for a cause for them outside ourselves and when we blame other persons or circumstances for making us feel what we feel. We then view ourselves as victims of what others do or say. We may even treat ourselves at the same time as victims of our own feelings. We intensify whatever feelings of helplessness or inadequacy have carried over from childhood. We then begin to judge and condemn ourselves for our feelings. We label our feelings as "bad," implying that they are morally wrong. We tell ourselves that we "shouldn't feel" hurt, or that we have no right to the anger that we feel. From there it is a short step to using our own feelings as the basis for judging another person to be wrong or bad. Our feelings may then provide the rationale and the energy for manipulating or attacking another person, or, if our tendency is to respond defensively rather than aggressively, we may simply avoid the other person.

In whatever way we devalue our own feelings, we diminish our capacity to be responsive. When we diminish the value of our own feelings, we are likely at the same time to devalue the feelings of others and thereby diminish our capacity to be responsive to them.

When we affirm our own feelings as expressions of who we are in response to events and/or people, we have no need to blame either ourselves or others on the basis of our feelings; neither do we need to fear the feelings of others. There is no need to avoid others or place ourselves under their judgment or submit to their control because of their feelings. Instead, we are free to discover the inherent value in whatever it is that we feel or that another person feels. Feelings thus become a window to the soul, a way of understanding ourselves and others. Our feelings become a means toward intimacy with others rather than a tool for manipulating them.

Our feelings function like an inner barometer. Just as a barometer measures the surrounding air pressure, our feelings register and measure the significance to us of what is happening in our lives. What I feel hurt by or angry at or afraid of will reflect the value or importance that I attach to that concern, event, or person. What comes to expression in such feeling responses, therefore, is an indication of who I am as the individual I am. Just as a barometer is functioning properly and is not "faulty" when it "falls," so my negative feelings are never wrong or sinful in themselves. Only what I *do* as a result of these feelings can be identified as morally right or wrong.

The negative feelings that we experience–hurt, anger, and fear in all their variations–can also be compared to negative film in pre-digital photography. Negatives are not much fun to look at for very long. But when we process and develop the negatives appropriately, they will produce positive prints. Valuing the positive prints, we can set aside the negatives, making use of them later only if we should want additional prints from them; they can then be processed once again. In the meantime, we'll enjoy the prints and show them to our friends.

If I process and develop my negative feelings appropriately, they will always produce a "picture" of what I value or consider important, and therefore of who I am. It may take time, but when I am ready I can move from the negative feeling to what the feeling reveals is of positive importance to me. I can go forward with a heightened awareness of what is of value to me. I can then leave behind the negative feeling, for it has served its purpose well. That is what is meant by "working through" a feeling. If, for example, someone slanders me or calls me names, I may feel deeply hurt and angry. These feelings are not a sign that I have been "damaged" by the slander; they are an indication that I value being respected, and consider such respect essential to a good relationship. Eventually, I may move from the hurt and angry feelings to a keener awareness of what I value as a human being. Old feelings from the past, like old negatives, can always be processed anew in the same way.

Feelings are never a problem in themselves. Feelings always have value. Problems arise only when we become "stuck" in our feelings and fail to work them through to an affirmation of what is important to us. Stuck in anger, we become resentful and bitter. Stuck in hurt, we become self-pitying. Stuck in fear, we may have panic attacks or phobias. We become stuck in feelings when we use them as weapons to attack someone or when we overprotect ourselves from possible hurt.

The more I move from negative feelings to the positive values which they reveal, the greater becomes my capacity to respond to myself with self-respect and to others with equal respect. Such respect creates the possibility of love. An appreciation of my individuality grows as I learn to affirm and value all of my feelings. The more I am able to affirm my own feelings the more responsive I will be to others with their feelings. We will take a further look at feelings as we consider in succeeding chapters the varying relationships that are important to us.

The Affirmation of Values

I grow in the sense of my individual worth when I respond to life by freely embracing moral and religious values. However, when I treat my embrace of such values as though they do not belong to my own responsiveness to others and to God, I restrict my moral and religious sensitivity rather than promote its growth. There are two basic ways in which I may do this.

The first way is to treat morality and spirituality as if they are simply matters of personal taste and nothing more. These values then have no reference to who other human beings are in their humanness, or to who God is in his divine sovereignty. I thus reduce all moral and religious values to mere subjectivism and relativism. The values that I embrace amount to nothing more than what suits me. I make myself, and nothing beyond me, the measure of what is or is not of value to me. In this way I reenact the original sin by making myself the measure of good and evil. I may not directly impose my values on others, but by making my values purely subjective I imply that others have no intrinsic worth as far as I am concerned. Total relativism will invariably limit my capacity to respond in love and with respect toward other human beings who differ from me in who they are and what they value. It also treats God as unimportant in himself, and thus limits my responsivity toward him.

The second way in which I might restrict moral and religious development would be to treat the values which I embrace as though they are absolutes, and not a part of my own responsiveness to other human beings and to God. The appeal to absolute values does embody an affirmation of the importance of moral and religious truths, but by treating these values as absolutes I place myself beyond accountability. I deny, in this case, that something of who I am comes to expression in the values I embrace. Thus I deprive myself (and others) of the opportunity to grow in an understanding of who I am as a moral and spiritual person. Genuine and open discussion of moral issues is then discouraged. An appeal to absolutes also puts me in a position where I inescapably judge others by my own values. In doing so, I will restrict rather than enhance my ability to know, understand, and care about the other person—or myself. I will tend to place others and myself under "the tyranny of the should." As I encounter other cultures different from my own I will have difficulty appreciating them in so far as I measure them by what I consider my own absolute values. Again, I reenact the original sin by making my values the measure of good and evil. An appeal to absolutes is a form of idolatry or "circumcision" that restricts moral and religious responsiveness. God alone is absolute.

Between the gods of relativism and the goddess of absolutism lies the affirmation that moral and religious values are an integral part of our human responsiveness to other human beings and to God. By embracing moral and religious commitments I am giving expression to who I am. But that is a discovery I make not in a vacuum. It is made in response both to a sovereign God and to other human beings who are like me and yet all very different from me. Being fully responsive to others precludes reducing moral assertions to a matter of personal taste; it also precludes simplistic moral judgments based on what are assumed to be absolutes. In my affirmation of moral values I am always dealing with my own response to other human beings. As I listen to the word of God in Scripture, I respond to what I hear by expressing something of who I am.

The Affirmation of Creativity

There is much more to life than feelings, more even than moral and religious values. To recognize responsivity as belonging to the core of our humanness is to recognize all the possibilities of living creatively in a redeemed world.

Creativity comes to expression in poetic and artistic works, in literature, in music, in dance, painting, and sculpture. It comes to expression in technical enterprises such as architecture and engineering, in woodworking, and in all the trades. Human creativity comes to expression in all the sciences, in medicine, and in philosophy. Politics and preaching provide arenas for creative activity, as do teaching and doing therapy and even writing theology. And so do the worlds of business and industry. Creativity comes into play in the daily rearing of children and the building of family and other relationships, as it does also in the formation of a worshiping community, and in playfulness, and in making love.

The more freely all such creativity comes to expression, the more God delights in us and is glorified by us. Freed from our fallen obsession with having to be right to be acceptable, we who bear the image of God are free to respond to God's redeemed world with all the creative imagination at our disposal.

The Affirmation of the Single Life

To see human responsivity as belonging to the core of our individuality is to recognize the single life as inherently worthy of affirmation. Much of life in society and in the church centers around married couples and their families. Singles, whether unmarried, divorced, or widowed, often feel neglected or left out. That is not surprising, considering that the majority still prefer to be married, and that most of us tend to measure others by ourselves.

Yet all of us were single at one time, and many of us, though once married, will again become single. Those who are divorced or widowed sometimes feel, at least for a time, that life has lost its real meaning. It can be an uphill struggle, sometimes taking years, to reclaim the worth of one's life as single.

Marriage is one significant context or relationship in which our human responsivity can develop and grow, but it is certainly not the only one, even for those who are married or may be parents. Because responsivity belongs to our individuality, the single life, too, offers unlimited opportunities for one's redeemed humanness to express itself in living responsively and creatively. What's more, the married and the single also have the opportunity to live responsively in relation to each other, and thus to grow in those relationships as well.

The Affirmation of Sexuality

Sexuality is at the core of our humanness. Created in the image of God, we were created sexual, as male and female. Everything I experience in life is filtered for me through my masculinity, as everything you experience may be filtered through your being female. All human relationships, whether with the opposite or with the same gender, have a sexual component to them. Because responsivity is a basic aspect of our individuality, every one of us will inescapably experience a component of sexual awareness in our responses to others.

Our sexual responsiveness is damaged either by excessive guilt and shame or by wanton promiscuity. Both guilt and promiscuity arise out of the experience of broken trust, and serve to impede the rebuilding of trust and the enjoyment of sexual responsiveness.

Guilt and shame over our sexual responsivity may arise from childhood sexual abuse; they may also come from subtle and powerful negative messages about our sexuality, and our natural childhood and adolescent curiosity about our sexual bodies. We easily learn to distrust our sexual responsiveness and our capacity to express it responsibly, learning to fear it, to feel guilt and shame over it, and to suppress the awareness and enjoyment of ourselves as sexual beings.

Promiscuity also restricts our capacity for a healthy expression and enjoyment of our sexuality. Promiscuity involves seeking sexual experience for its own sake, without building a relationship of trust. A sexual affair by one who is married breaks the bond of trust. Not that the sex involved is "dirty" or "ugly;" the sex may be as delicious and even as nourishing as the "apple" in Eden, but it will just as surely destroy trust.

In a world redeemed by God, we can learn increasingly to affirm, experience, and manage our sexual responsiveness in ways that cultivate and express trust. Then we will also celebrate and enhance our growth as sexual individuals.

The Affirmation of Spirituality

Human responsivity comes to expression through our feelings, in our embracing of moral and religious values, in all the various forms of human creativity, in single as well as married life, and in our sexuality. Beneath all of these, however, lies the deeper core of our spirituality.

Spirituality expresses itself in many ways. For some its expression is largely emotional; for others it is primarily moral; for still others its focus is intellectual. Spirituality takes shape in formal religious exercises for many. Whatever form it takes, spirituality is the seeking of meaning for our lives within some community of acceptance and love. As one Reformation formulation (the Heidelberg Catechism) asks at the outset, "What is your only comfort in life and in death?" That is, what is the deepest underlying concern in your life: What is it that you most want to be assured of as you live your life and as you face death? The stated answer is "That I belong...." Created to be responsive, we who bear God's image have an insatiable desire to belong. Yet our deepest fear is always that we do not really belong because something is not right with us—or with others, if we're into blaming.

That spiritual core, the desire to belong, is present in all human beings. It is at the root of the tension between our individuality and our yearning to be in relationships where we do belong. In the deepest roots of our being, we want to experience that we are significant to others and valued by them as we, in turn, make them significant to us and value them.

And that occurs as we lay aside our obsession with determining who is right and who is wrong. It happens, we could say, as we are cleansed of original sin. It occurs when we begin to live and act, instead, within a circle of trust and love which nurtures individual growth and promotes the freedom to be creative intellectually and emotionally in all that we do. In relation both to God and to others, that freedom is the fruit of genuine spirituality.

Mental and Emotional Illness

When we recognize the spiritual dimension that underlies all mental and emotional problems that individuals experience, we can also identify why it is that certain kinds of spiritual answers given for emotional difficulties often make problems worse rather than proving helpful.

Healthy emotional/mental development requires an environment of trust. Newborn infants need to develop the trust that they will be fed when hungry and tended to when uncomfortable; they need to be able to trust that their basic needs will be met and that they will be loved. The growing child needs to develop the trust that even when limits are set for him, his parents care about him and value his feelings, ideas, interests, and abilities. The adolescent who is gradually moving toward independence needs to experience a trust from his parents that includes not only unquestioned love but also confidence in his emerging adulthood. The infant, the child, and the adolescent all need to develop and grow up within a circle of trust and love, in the family and in a wider community, if each is to develop a healthy mental and emotional sense of self. Each child needs to know—not just by being told, but through experiencing it—what it means to belong.

Who of us as children experienced this sense of belonging as fully as we needed? Who of us as parents have provided our children with as full a measure of that spiritual nourishment as they required? Who of us is without some emotional struggles and pain?

The spiritual root of all emotional problems is the inability to trust. Emotional problems emerge when trust breaks down instead of being nourished. Instead of learning to trust, we learn how to "be good" and to "be right," how to be competent and to achieve—and thus to measure up. These, we learn, are the way to become and to feel accepted, and to experience belonging. And, like the "apple" in Eden, these are all good things. It is good to be good. It is good to be right. It is also good to be competent and to achieve. But when these good things take the place of trust and love and are made the basis for being accepted and for belonging, seeds are being sown for emotional enslavement. When these good things are imposed from outside a circle of trust and love they become the source of emotional and mental problems.

Anxiety in its various forms—chronic and diffused, or acute as in panic attacks or phobias—involves the underlying fear that something is not "right" with me. Something keeps me from being acceptable. Some shame within keeps me from being good enough to belong. That is our "original fear" which has displaced original trust. Often that fear leads to an addiction—to alcohol, to drugs, to gambling, to food, to work, to sex, and even to religion.

Shame leads to family secrets that create more fear. Family patterns coming from shame result in blocking growth, and are often perpetuated from one generation to another.

In anxiety there is still hope. But when hope of being good enough fades, we despair and become depressed. Depression in its various degrees of severity goes deeper than just a fear of not being "right." We begin really to believe that we will never be good enough or right enough to belong.

A highly anxious person or a deeply depressed person is usually someone who experienced significant deprivation of trust and belonging in growing up. Such deprivation may come from subtle but persistent forms of abuse or neglect. The same result may come from physical abuse, or from severe emotional abuse—from frequently being called names or from constantly being told that "you'll never amount to anything." Such deprivation may come through being sexually abused (at least one-third of those I see in therapy, men as well as women, have been sexually abused). Homes in which one or both parents are alcoholic provide a good seedbed for emotional problems in the children, problems that will carry over well into adulthood.

Abuse that is persistent may give rise to personality disorders. Personality disorders involve anxiety and depression, but they also involve much more. The whole personality can organize itself around certain patterned ways of thinking about oneself and forming expectations of others that become rigid. This rigidity interferes with developing healthy relationships. All the various personality disorders involve a breakdown in developing the capacity to trust. In place of trust comes a distorted focus on being good or being right. The resulting disorder rigidly limits the capacity of the individual to be responsive in relationships with others.

The individual with an "obsessive-compulsive" personality disorder, for example, has developed a pattern of thinking in which he sees nearly all issues in terms of being right or wrong. Everything is a matter of black and white. Such a person does not see or pay attention to all the colors of the rainbow that lie between black and white. He will invest a great deal of energy in determining just what is right. He will then try equally hard to convince others that he is right and that they, if they differ from him, are wrong. He has little capacity to listen to, let alone understand or value, the concerns of others. His responsive capacities are so limited that he will develop little intimacy with others.

The "narcissistic" personality is so convinced that everything is right with him that he feels he is consistently entitled to the accolades of others. In contrast, the "avoidant" personality is so convinced that she is unacceptable and does not belong that she will avoid as much social interaction and closeness with others as possible. One who suffers from a "paranoid" personality disorder fears so deeply that he does not belong that he suspects others of being out to hurt him at every turn. The deepest spiritual root of all these psychiatric conditions involves the breakdown of trust. A concern with being right or good takes the place of trusting.

The road to recovery and health always involves the discovery of new possibilities for trusting. And because Christian faith at its core is a call to trust, holding to and growing in that faith provides a powerful resource for any individual who is on the road to recovery from anxiety, from depression, from one of the personality disorders, or from an adjustment reaction (for example, to the loss of a marriage or a job).

If all psychiatric problems are at root spiritual problems, why not get right down to that root by calling individuals with such problems to simply have more faith and to pray and trust and read their Bibles more faithfully? From a Christian perspective, should not people with those kinds of emotional problems be directly confronted with their sins, including that of not having enough faith? Should they not be called to repentance instead of to one or another form of psychological exploration or the use of medication?

The difficulty with that approach, popular though it is in certain Christian communities, is that it reenacts the drama of subtle temptation that originally occurred in the Garden of Eden. It treats such good "apples" as faith, prayer, Bible reading, and repentance as if these are the spiritual acts that we must do, and do right and good enough, if we are to gain wisdom and emotional health. Like the subtle serpent in Eden's garden, naïve or deceptive practitioners of religious mental health cures offer "instant wisdom"—do these spiritual exercises, and your eyes will be opened! You will become wise, emotionally healthy, in no time at all if you just do it right yourself!

The difficulty is that the person who is anxious to begin with will likely generate more anxiety, and the depressed person more depression, and the obsessive person more obsessions still, as they now struggle to get it all just right spiritually—and fail, time and time again. The risk is that they will now become more convinced than ever that they do not belong—to God or to anyone else—and that God is surely against them as much as angry or distant Daddy was.

What these individuals (like all of us) need is someone who is for them, as God is. They need someone who will embody—not lecture about—the grace of a God who calls us home to himself. They need a trusted friend, an understanding pastor, or an empathetic support group. What they really need is a supportive and trusting community of people who will uphold them and walk with them through their fears and in their pain. That is what the church is called to be—a community of faith, where trust grows because it is experienced without judgment and condemnation. With all their fears and sadness and inadequacies, broken people need assurance that together with us they do indeed belong to God.

In many cases they need encouragement to seek professional therapy from a competent Christian counselor. Whether counseling takes one or two meetings, ten sessions, or ten or more years is not what matters most. What matters most is that they have the understanding of a dear friend, a caring counselor, and a Christian community—a context that allows them, at their own pace, to openly explore their fears, their anger, their grief, and their pain as meaningful windows to their very selves. Counseling that is Christian provides a context of grace in which individuals are enabled to explore the pain they are stuck in, pain that often has roots in the families in which they grew up.

Emotional pain and mental stress often take their toll on the body with its complex physiological processes. Those processes, some of which occur in the brain and regulate mood and emotional stability, inevitably vary from one individual to another. They also appear to be influenced by genetic inheritance. Though they are part of the resources with which we are born, they may also limit our human responsiveness. Some of us have a chemical-physiological makeup that is more vulnerable to stress than that which others inherit. To make use of medications to modify anxiety and depression, where indicated, is far from a denial of Christian faith, as some imply. On the contrary, the use of medications may simply mean that I accept my particular life in all its facets as a gift from God; though disturbed by sin and the brokenness of the world, yet restored—not by my moral or religious works, but as a gift of grace.

Summary

Much of the stress we experience in our lives involves a tension between our individual interests and the growth of relationships that are important to us. Responsivity belongs to the core of our individuality, but we cannot escape the limitations imposed on us by our finitude and our fears. We also discover that our growth as individuals involves the affirmation of our own responsiveness in all areas of our lives—in our feelings, in our moral and religious values, in all areas of human creativity, and in our sexuality, whether as married or as single. Underlying all of these is the affirmation of spirituality as a yearning to belong—to belong to a trusting community of people and ultimately to a faithful and gracious God. Emotional illness arises when trust that we do belong is destroyed and is replaced by an obsessive concern over our being right or good enough to merit belonging.

We turn now to the other side of the coin. Our individuality itself, in its responsive character, drives us to seek out and create relationships—in marriage, in raising a family, in joining a church, and in living in a community and broader society where we work and play. How can a perspective on renewed human responsivity in a redeemed world enable us to live and grow responsively within these various relationships?

7

LIVING RESPONSIVELY in
MARRIAGE

More than half of American marriages last until death separates. Of those marriages that endure, many appear to be reasonably satisfying. Fewer than half end in divorce. I find that to be encouraging for marriage as an institution. What is more, many of those who have been divorced or who are widowed are eventually willing and even eager to enter into a marital relationship again. Others who have been hurt too deeply to risk another legalized marriage still live together in a quasi-marital state, and some of these do eventually decide to solemnize their relationship.

I can easily imagine a world in which men and women had become so self-centered and shallow, so hurt and angry and distrustful, and so fearful of any commitment, that no one would stay in a marriage for long, and few would enter to begin with. Everyone would seek to get their own immediate needs met at the moment as best they could, in whatever way possible. In such a world, where trust is destroyed and the capacity to be responsive in love is extinguished, no one could count on anything from anyone.

Thank God, we don't live in such a world. Our world has been loved and redeemed by God. His promise, his commitment, renews our capacity to be responsive in love—love toward God and toward each other with commitment. While it is understandable that some have become disillusioned with marriage, and fearful of making any lasting commitment, it remains possible for many others to build an enduring marital relationship.

Possible—but seldom easy, and probably never without some risk and struggle. Even in the best of marriages there are times when each spouse has fantasies of being free of the other. Commitment is what carries a relationship through the rough times until the warmth of love and affection is renewed.

Commitment is to a marriage what a skeleton is to the body; commitment gives form and shape and enduring structure to a relationship. But commitment is not enough. Who would want to embrace a bare skeleton? Love, warmth, and affection are the flesh and blood of a relationship, but who would want to embrace a limp and floppy body that had no inner skeleton? Few relationships can endure without the strength of skeletal commitment, but no relationship can endure and be enjoyed only on the bare bones of commitment. The skeleton of commitment needs the flesh and blood of responsive warmth and love to bring it alive.

In Search of a New Model

Many of us grew up with a model for marriage and family that can be called hierarchical or authoritarian. That model has been operative with countless variations in most societies of the world throughout the history of humankind. Most religious systems have endorsed some form of it. Christian writers, too, have had no difficulty enlisting biblical support for this model. In doing so, many have given the hierarchical model a normative status, endowing it with divine authority. This model then presumes to tell us what a marriage "should be" if it is to be truly Christian.

The problem is that the Scriptures provide no ready-made model for marriage. They give us no prescription on how a courtship is to be conducted or how a marriage between two persons is to be developed. They give examples of how some marriages were arranged, like that of Isaac to Rebekah, Jacob first to Leah and then to Rachel, David to Bathsheba, among others, and Solomon with this many wives and concubines. Nowhere, however, is the quality of a marriage explicitly analyzed in the Scriptures. Even in the New Testament we receive only some terse principles and a metaphor or two.

When we construct a model for marriage and family life, therefore, it is always one of our own making. Any model that we adopt and make use of will be one that involves our own responsiveness both to the message of the Scriptures and to relationships as we know and understand them. But such a model will not itself be prescriptive or possess any inherent authority. It will always be subject to revision. Think of the many ways in which the hierarchical model itself has been altered in different times and cultures throughout history.

Why then should we look for a model for marriage and family? The answer is simply that such a model may be useful. It may give us a reference point by which to identify some of the ongoing issues that contemporary marriages face, and provide a framework in which to raise or recognize the kind of issues that a marriage today will be dealing with. A good model will enable us to ask ourselves from time to time, "How are we doing?" It will identify the parameters within which a good marriage will function best, outside of which problems are likely to emerge.

Christians will be best served by a model that both comes out of their Christian faith and at the same time helps them give further expression to that faith within their marriages and families. Moreover, if such a model is truly useful it will serve Christians of all persuasions and even, perhaps, those who are not professing Christians and do not accept the faith assumptions involved in the model.

Let's look first at the traditional hierarchical model and then at an alternative model, a Trinitarian model, which may be helpful for understanding and building marital and family life.

The Hierarchical Model

The hierarchical model for marriage and family takes as its primary focus a concern with authority. It seeks to express and maintain a proper ordering of authority. Within marriage a couple's calling is to uphold that proper ordering of authority, and for Christians the order of authority is set in a broader context that includes God, Christ, and the rest of the world. In the Christianized hierarchical model the proper ordering of authority that is to be upheld is the following:

God
Christ
Husband
Wife
Child
Animals and earth

Here God is seen as having the highest, or sovereign, power and authority. Christ is under God's authority and submissive to God, but Christ has authority over the husband, who must be submissive to Christ; the husband, in turn, has authority over his wife, who must be submissive to him. The wife possesses authority over the children, but in exercising that authority she is still subject to the authority of her husband. The child is subject to the mother and to the father and to Christ and to God. Within that authority structure all human beings, as image-bearers of God, have dominion over the rest of creation.

What is not clear is to what extent this model can also be applied to human relationships outside of marriage, as in the church and in society. Many today restrict its application to marriage and the family. Others attempt to extend it to the church but not to society. Still others try to maintain the notion that in all of society all men have authority over all women.

Within marriage and the family, however, this model can function to identify what its proponents consider to be the primary tasks of a husband and a wife. They are each to maintain their proper places and fulfill their roles within the authority and power structure that is presumed to have originated from creation. This structure sets the parameters within which a happy and blessed marriage and family life is believed to flourish.

This hierarchical model with its authority structure also identifies the parameters outside of which we may expect problems and difficulties to arise, either when the husband neglects to exercise his proper authority, or when the wife or the children take to themselves an authority which does not belong to them but belongs to the husband. When a married couple using this model asks, "How are we doing?" they will be asking how well the husband is maintaining and exercising his authority and whether the wife is sufficiently and appropriately submissive to him.

One implication of this model is that a husband is entrusted with the responsibility to restrict the role and the personal growth of his wife and children by his own exercise of authority. While he may promote their growth in many ways, he must nonetheless ensure that they do not claim for themselves what rightfully belongs only to him. This model also limits the possibilities of a husband's learning submission to his wife as part of his responsiveness to her. The wife is expected to limit the responsibilities that she takes on herself for leadership in the relationship. The hierarchical model for marriage tends to restrict rather than to expand the responsiveness of each to the other.

When a husband for whatever reason does not assert his authority, the wife is put in an uncomfortable situation. She may need to take over and become the dominant one for the sake of the family, contrary to this model; or, she may try to get her husband to do what she wants him to do, namely, to display real authority and exercise decisive leadership. She may even claim that she has divine authority behind her urgings. But, if the husband begins to do what she wants him to do, who is really in control? Who is then being submissive to whom?

In one of the couples I encountered, I was told by the wife that before marriage she and her husband had both agreed that they would have an entirely egalitarian marriage. Some years after marrying, however, she came under the influence of a charismatic religious group which insisted that God's will is that the husband should be in control. She decided that it was now necessary that her husband make all final decisions in their relationship; he, however, resisted doing so. Somehow she could not see that if her husband would accede to her new demands he would be acknowledging her right unilaterally to redefine the nature of their marital relationship—she would thereby control its direction. In this case the husband became more and more depressed and increasingly turned to alcohol. He could no more find a constructive way to respond to her than she could to him.

No model for marriage can be expected to resolve all problems within a marriage. Models do not prevent or solve problems. However, the model we unconsciously or consciously adopt for marriage will influence the focus we give to our relationship. It will determine the kind of concerns to which we become sensitive. The hierarchical model for marriage makes us sensitive to the issue of who is in control and who must be submissive; beyond that, this model gives very little guidance. The role of love in such a marriage is not derived from the model but must be imported from somewhere else. The paradox is that the more loving and Christ-like a husband is, the less the hierarchical model will serve any function within the marriage, whereas a tyrannical and abusive husband and father can claim to be following this model.

Clearly we need a new model for marriage, one that will serve us better and will reflect Christian faith more broadly.

A Trinitarian Model

The Christian doctrine of the Trinity offers us a potentially helpful model for understanding and assessing human relationships in general, and for developing marital and family life in particular. As an alternative to the hierarchical model, a model based on the Trinity offers several distinct advantages. Because the doctrine of the Trinity is almost universally accepted among Christians, and belongs close to the heart of the Christian faith, we may hope to discover some inherent connection between our faith and our marriages, such that each will reinforce the rich meaning of the other.

A model based on the Trinity will draw on a broad range of biblical material. All the principles we discovered in creation and in our being formed in the image of the Triune God (see chapter 2) are relevant. We may even discover that sin and redemption can be talked about in relation to marriage in a way that is helpful rather than being either threatening or overly idealistic. If that potential is realized, marital and family life will be enriched by our faith in the Triune God; at the same time our experience of marriage and family relationships can enrich our understanding of a Creator-God who is one yet three, and three yet fully one. (And if we discover that the same model is helpful for relationships in the church and in all of society, so much the better!)

Let's begin with the central mystery of the Trinity. God is one God. Yet God is Father, Son, and Holy Spirit. Three distinct persons are nonetheless one God. In Christian thought, neither the oneness of God nor the distinctness of the three persons is to be compromised, nor is one of the persons subordinated to another; each person has its own identity within the unity. Laying aside any compulsion to explain the mystery, we can open ourselves to experience reflections of that mystery in our human relationships.

As we discussed in chapter 2, by sovereign creative power and out of his own inner imagining, a triune God forms responsive creatures who are empowered to have dominion. The mystery of the Godhead is reflected in the image-bearer: one "adam" who is both singular and plural, distinct as male and female, yet wholly one in their humanness. Here, within human relationships, we most poignantly experience the mystery of the One whom we image.

In marriage two distinctly different persons, one female and one male, each with their own individual personality and life history, become one. And yet they remain two. The unity does not destroy the distinctness. The distinctness does not mar the oneness. To develop a balance between being one and being two is the never-ending task of every good marriage.

A Trinitarian model for marriage helps identify this central issue that underlies all other issues in a marriage: the recognition of and respect for the distinctiveness of each partner in the marriage, while both share the dominion given to "adam" ("the human one") at the time of creation. Thus our concern is not with one partner's having to maintain authority for himself while the other partner alone learns to be submissive. In this model concern is not with authority, but with the responsiveness that empowers ongoing personal growth for both spouses individually and for the marital union at the same time. In short, two guiding principles promote the growth of a successful Christian marriage: (1) respect for the distinct personhood and individual growth of each spouse, and (2) concern with enhancing the bonding or unity between the two spouses.

On the surface, and often in practice, these two seem to contradict and work against each other. "Has my own identity been lost through marriage?" she wonders. While he muses (or fumes), "If my wife keeps getting more independent and self-sufficient, will she still need me and want the marriage?" The mystery of what makes a growing and rewarding marital relationship lies in the working out together of these two seemingly opposite concerns.

When a husband and wife stand back and assess their marriage with this Trinitarian model in mind, the question "How are we doing?" takes on new significance. The parameters within which a healthy marriage develops are now identified as including both the individual growth of each partner and, at the same time, the growth of oneness between the two spouses.

Each spouse does well to ask at times, "How am I doing? Am I relating to my spouse in ways that promote the development of his/her personality gifts, sense of self, sense of accomplishment?

And (just as important) am I continuing to develop myself as an individual?" In the Trinitarian model, it is important for each to also maintain an awareness of how their respective development as individuals is at the same time promoting the growth of their marital relationship, the oneness between them.

The Trinitarian model likewise identifies the parameters outside of which a marital relationship is likely to deteriorate. This can happen in one of two ways.

First, a marriage is likely to get into difficulty when one or each of the partners is primarily seeking his or her own individual direction, interests, or development without genuine regard for the effect on the other spouse or on the relationship as a whole. As some in the family systems movement would say, such a couple's marriage can be characterized as "disengaged."

Second, a marriage will suffer when oneness or togetherness is imposed by one on the other without due regard for the individual interests or needs of each spouse. Often there is a supposition that each of the spouses should think and feel and desire the same things; the one is seen as an extension of the other. Such a marriage is sometimes termed "enmeshed."

Opposite as they appear, a common thread runs through both kinds of dysfunctional marriages. What characterizes each of these types of marriages is the lack of genuine responsiveness to each other. In the first instance, one's own development is pursued quite apart from being responsive to the other spouse and to the growth of unity in the marriage. In the second instance, unity or togetherness in the marriage is rigorously pursued without a genuine responsiveness to each other as individuals who have distinct personalities, interests, needs, talents, and goals.

Now, with this Trinitarian model in mind, we can explore at greater length some of the other primary issues involved in building a healthy marriage as we live responsively in relation to each other.

Togetherness and Separateness

In every marriage the basic challenge that underlies and runs through all other issues is that of creating a satisfactory blend of togetherness and separateness. We could also call it a balance between marital unity and individuality, or between dependence and independence, or between closeness and distance. The tensions that inevitably occur within a marriage will have something to do with the tension found inherent in this remarkable polarity.

It is relatively easy for "experts" on marriage to write how-to books that tell us just how to work out our marriages in this regard. But experts do not build our marriages. Two individuals, with all the differences that separate them, are the ones seeking to build a new union in marriage; each marriage will be built out of the individual "stuff" that each of the two partners is made of. For that reason prescriptions for marriage are necessarily general, as no two marriages will ever be the same.

What we can do, however, is to identify those issues that all of us as human beings will face in building a satisfying marital relationship. And perhaps we can make some observations about how the two poles of togetherness and separateness, dependence and independence, can interact with each other constructively. Let's first notice some of the varied contexts in which the issue of togetherness versus separateness arises.

Time and Space

In the most literal sense, a couple needs to find time to spend together in the same space. But the individual spouses will likely each have some need for time alone, some desire for "having my own space." One wife complained to me that her husband insisted on following her to whatever room she went in the house, even wanting to be with her in the bathroom every time she went there. Another wife commented that her husband insisted that she sit outdoors with him while he changed the oil in his car or made other repairs. I also know a wife who will not let her husband out of her sight at any public gathering.

Each spouse needs some moments of privacy. But how much of a couple's leisure, entertainment, and cultural activity is engaged in together, and how much does each do alone? To what extent do they share friends and family together? And how much does she spend evenings out with her own friends and family, and he with his? Are holidays and vacations always shared, or sometimes spent separately? And if shared, are the two always doing things together, or is some time apart needed even when vacationing? If so, does each need roughly the same amount of time alone?

What happens when one spouse is expecting togetherness at a time when the other is needing his or her own space? The spouse who is wanting closeness is likely to feel rejected, abandoned, unloved, devalued, or unimportant. And the spouse who needs time alone but is pressured to be together is likely to feel manipulated, controlled, smothered, and misunderstood. These are the issues that every marriage needs to work out.

Role Definitions

The issue of togetherness and separateness will also enter into the working out of gender roles within the marriage. Here the question is not just a matter of being spatially close or apart for a time. It also concerns a husband's and a wife's expectations regarding what tasks will be done individually and which will be shared. Will the two share equally in the responsibility for providing sufficient income to meet the family's needs, or will one have greater responsibility as provider? And to what extent will household chores—cooking, cleaning, laundry, choosing furniture, deciding on interior decorations, maintaining the upkeep of the house and yard and automobiles—be seen as the mutual responsibility of husband and wife together, or be divided between them separately? How and on what basis will the division of tasks be accomplished? To what extent will the raising and care of children be shared or divided? Are the measures of discipline determined and carried out separately, he in his way and she in hers, or are these worked out together? Who is expected to attend school functions and parent-teacher conferences, one spouse alone, or both together?

The Sexual Relationship

At first glance we might suppose that the sexual relationship belongs wholly on the togetherness side of the polarity, representing the mutual desire for closeness. Yet even here the issue of togetherness and separateness is present in significant ways.

The main issue here is to what extent spouses can recognize that each of them possesses his and her own distinct sexuality as part of each one's individuality. Each of them has had his and her own history of sexual development and coming to awareness that has shaped sexual attitudes. The kinds of sexual inhibitions each has will reflect the personal history and growth of each one. The spouses not only have distinctly different sexual organs, but their ways of responding erotically, both physically and emotionally, will differ for each of them in the marriage. What the entire experience of intercourse as "making love" means will be personal to each. It will also vary from one occasion or context to another.

What is more, how the whole tone of everything else in the marital relationship affects the desire and readiness for intercourse may be quite different for each of them. A heated argument may stimulate for the one a desire for coming close in making love; the same argument may provoke a need for greater distance in the other. What they desire immediately after intercourse may also be quite different; she may wish to cuddle for a time, he to fall asleep at once. How frequently each desires intercourse may also differ. The timing and mood on any one occasion may differ, as may the desire for variety and experimentation. How each feels about stimulation to orgasm apart from intercourse—alone, with, or by the other—may vary considerably. Each may have private sexual fantasies and dreams, which may or may not be shared.

In addition, because each as an individual is inherently sexual, the wife will have her way of responding in everyday interactions to others of the opposite sex, and the husband will have his way of doing so. How one spouse reacts to the other's finding someone else attractive may also reflect distinctly individual traits.

Thus, in the sexual relationship within marriage, the central and challenging concern is always to respect the individual distinctness of each spouse, even while cultivating at the same time a deepening bond of sexual union in the relationship.

The Management of Money

The issue of togetherness and separateness also influences the way in which a couple manage their finances. How each handles money is very much an expression of who each one is as an individual. Every marriage faces the challenge of giving due respect to the individual traits of each spouse that affect his and her use of money, while at the same time attempting to forge a sense of togetherness in this area.

One question here involves how decisions about spending are made. Does each spouse make his or her own spending decisions independently of the other, or are all decisions made together? Does the amount of income earned by a spouse determine how much influence that spouse has in how the money is spent, or are such decisions made together regardless of who has earned the money? Is all earned income placed in a common "pot" or account, with equal access by each? Or does each have a separate account? Even with a common account, does one or each have a private "kitty" on the side for special or personal purchases? Again, how are decisions made about spending versus saving, separately by one alone, or together by common consent? Money becomes an issue in a marriage either when one spouse spends too independently for the other's comfort, or when one spouse imposes dependency by enforcing restrictions that the other cannot live with.

Money has symbolic or emotional meanings that can be deeply rooted in an individual's personality and experiences in his or her family of origin. One spouse may be impulsive and the other more disciplined in personality. For one person, spending money may be associated with a need for love or for freedom or for just feeling important, whereas for another, saving money may represent a need for security or for control. In marriage the issue is whether a couple can create a style of managing money that successfully respects the individual personality traits and emotional needs of each while enhancing the sense of oneness between them as well.

Moral, Religious, and Cultural Values

In the broad arena of values, particularly those that require being acted on, the same issue of togetherness versus separateness arises. It is certainly advantageous for a married couple to have shared values, especially on moral and religious matters, but also in regard to cultural matters like music, art, theater, and other forms of entertainment. The same is true of special interests such as sports, hobbies, and volunteer work in the community, or an interest in history, the sciences, or travel.

Problems can quickly arise in a marriage where values are not shared. How much will one spouse seek to cajole the other into affirming or going along with his or her own wishes, thus coercing togetherness regarding values? How much difference in values can the marriage tolerate without destroying the union or impeding its growth?

The Interplay of Togetherness and Separateness

I often think of marriage as an arena which two individuals enter together. Each brings into this arena his or her own innate personality, shaped as each is by differing life histories in their respective families of origin. Each also has his or her own sexual identity and needs. And then, consciously or not, in some significant way each attempts to form a marriage and family that is compatible with one's own personality and similar to one's own family of origin. The husband tries to recreate his original family, and the wife hers. Marriage seems to be a natural setup for power struggles in which each spouse attempts to make the other conform to one's own needs and goals. Marriage is thus an excellent arena for each to reenact the original sin again and again. Each easily falls into making his or her own way of handling various issues the measure of what is good or bad, right or wrong.

The creative challenge of marriage is to take something of each individual and weave it together into a new whole. The resulting creation will not be a reproduction either of his or of her family of origin. The new creation is not simply an extension of who he is in his personality and sexuality, nor is it an extension of who she is in hers. It is a blending of her individuality and his into a new whole that does not destroy or even limit the individuality of either one, but enhances both wife and husband as the respective person each is.

It is possible for both sides of the unity-diversity polarity to develop and grow at the same time. Togetherness and separateness, closeness and distance, dependence and independence, growth in marital unity and development of individuality—both sides belong together in a creative tension. In a healthy marriage both sides will be growing at the same time. More than that, each side of the polarity will enhance the growth of the other.

Such a happy state of affairs may develop along these lines: The husband is responsive to and supportive of the individual needs of his wife. He encourages her in the pursuit of her interests and goals and in the expression of her feelings. As she experiences his support and encouragement, she will value her relationship to him in marriage all the more. And as the wife offers the same kind of support for the husband to be developing himself in his way at his own pace, he will, in turn, increasingly experience the marriage relationship as a source of strength and enrichment to him. As each supports and encourages individual growth in the other, respecting the need for distance and separateness at times, the bond in the marriage will also develop. At the same time, commitment to the developing marital bond will challenge each of the spouses to develop new and creative responses to each other that will constitute personal growth. In this way commitment to the marital union supports individual growth at the same time that individual development enhances the satisfaction that each finds in the marital union.

What seems to be at work in the process of a healthy, growing marital relationship is a principle similar to that which we found at work already in all the processes of creation (chapter 2). In the creative process, something new emerged at each step through a separation into two parts. In and by their separateness the two parts came together to form a new and enriched whole. Through this creative process each individual part was likewise enriched in its own identity. So it is also with God. Father, Son, and Holy Spirit each participate in distinct ways in creation and in redemption, such that one God is glorified through it all. This same process is at work in every healthy marriage.

In a broken world where trust has repeatedly been violated, the process described here for marriage never goes entirely smoothly. All too often it breaks down in unresolved conflict as each spouse makes oneself the measure of what is good. Let's move on to explore what it can mean for a married couple to live responsively in the midst of conflict, taking a look at how conflict can be turned into a constructive process of growth both for the marital relationship and for each spouse individually.

Dealing with Conflict Responsively

When married couples fight, they are always arguing over the same issue. The specific context of the fight may vary from one occasion to the next. That context may involve money one day, sex the next, and how strict or lenient to be with the children on still a third occasion. At other times it may involve whose parents to visit on Christmas Eve, or whether the husband has been drinking too much, or whether the wife is spending too much money. Sometimes the fight may center on personality traits, such as whether the husband is "always" thoughtless or the wife a "constant" nag. Or it may have to do with who said what during the last disagreement. But whatever the specific content, the issue of contention is always the same: *who is right and who is wrong.*

In every argument the husband is intent on proving that he is right and his wife is wrong, and the wife is equally intent on establishing that he is wrong and she is right. A variation on the same theme involves proving who is the good guy and who is the bad one. And you already know, of course, who the good guy is— whoever is speaking at the moment claims that honor for him- or herself. If a husband and wife are arguing and not just carrying on a rational discussion, you can count on the argument being over who is right and who is wrong, no matter what the particulars are about.

What's Wrong with Being Right in Marriage?

When we analyze what is occurring in all such arguments, we become aware that the spouses are responding to each other out of their respective hurt and angry feelings. Something has happened (or not happened) that leaves one or both feeling unloved, neglected, rejected, belittled, unimportant, devalued, manipulated, etc. As an argument progresses, four responsive ingredients are likely to be present:

1. Fear: When we have been hurt and are angry, we look ahead to the continuing future of our relationship, and we become afraid that the same hurt will occur again. This is a legitimate concern, of course; none of us wants to keep on being hurt. Or our fear may be that the relationship itself will dissolve. In the midst of conflict fear may well be a controlling factor as we each try to convince the other that we are right.

2. Hiding: Being afraid, we are not likely to disclose to each other much of our own inner feelings. We feel too vulnerable to be open. Arguing to prove that I am right and she is wrong is like putting on a fig leaf to cover and protect myself.

3. Blaming: As I set about to prove that I am right and my spouse is wrong, I will respond to the situation by blaming her. She will also blame me. We will be standing in judgment on each other, perhaps even condemning each other when the argument gets intense. Since there is usually more than enough blame to go

around, we will each probably be right in our blaming.

4. <u>Controlling</u>: Arguments usually involve some attempt to control each other. We are trying to get the other spouse to change his or her ways—to conform to our own preferences or insights or needs. Again, from our own point of view, we usually each have good reasons for wanting the other spouse to change.

In all of these maneuvers we are, in effect, each making our self the measure of what is good and right and true. By focusing on our being right and our spouse wrong, we are breaking down rather than building or rebuilding trust. We may be responding in a largely defensive manner or in a mainly aggressive way, or we may adopt a combination hit-and-run tactic. But in any case we will be reenacting the original sin within our marriage. The result is that in dealing with our conflicts we adopt responses to each other that limit rather than expand our capacity to grow responsively in relation to each other.

What's Right in a Marriage Gone Wrong?

A couple can learn to make one important shift in order to deal constructively with conflict in their marriage. They can shift away from trying to prove who's right and who's wrong. Instead they can move toward a growing discovery of "who's who?" Conflict within a marriage provides an opportunity for growth for both husband and wife. In conflict you can discover more of who you are; you may also discover more of who your spouse is. What is it that is coming to expression when you are in conflict and are experiencing deep hurt, intense anger, or numbing fear? The surfacing of these emotions is letting you know what issues are important to each of you—what, to you, is worth fighting about.

Whenever we give up the struggle to prove that we are right and our spouse is wrong, and instead turn conflict into a discovery of who each of us is, a whole new process emerges. The power struggles so typical of conflictual marriages diminish. Trust begins to grow again. Four new responsive ingredients will increasingly appear in the marital relationship:

1. <u>Confidence</u> in each other will begin to replace the fear.
2. <u>Openness</u> will grow in place of hiding and withholding.
3. <u>Understanding</u> will more and more displace the blaming.
4. <u>Cooperation</u> and creative compromise will replace control.

The capacity to be responsive to each other in marriage thus grows, and with it the marital bond grows as well. When one spouse fears, hides from, blames, or seeks to control the other, that spouse is distancing him- or herself from the other. Such a spouse communicates a diminishing of the other's worth. But when those responses are replaced by confidence, openness, understanding, and cooperation, each partner enhances the worth of the other, and the value of the marriage is increased in the eyes of both.

A marriage relationship grows best, of course, when husband and wife are mutually responsive to each other. But what happens when one spouse refuses to be responsive, persisting instead with blaming and withdrawing, and with efforts to control and diminish the other? The chances are that such a relationship will not last long; if it does, it will not be very satisfying for either one.

Still, even when your spouse persists in blaming and belittling, you do well to focus on developing your own capacity to respond. You need not limit your responses to those of the same kind. Your energy does not need to go into blaming and trying to change your spouse. Here are a few suggestions that may help you to expand your own responsivity:

1. Summarize in your own words what your spouse is saying. When you are attacked or belittled, the two most natural things for you to do are to defend yourself and to attack back. Instead, try to sum up fairly what you understand your spouse to be saying.

2. Ask Further Questions about the judgments, attitudes, ideas, feelings, needs, and desires of your spouse. Allowing your spouse to be accountable for his or her own attitudes and feelings is a way of refusing to let yourself be placed under your spouse's judgments.

3. Focus on the Feelings beneath the judgments. When your spouse is attacking you, you have a choice. You can agree that you are the issue and therefore respond defensively or by attacking back, or you can assume that your spouse is talking about her- or himself, and that your spouse's feelings express something of who he or she is (and not who you are).

4. Highlight the Differences between yourself and your spouse. Keep in mind that the issue is not who is right and who is wrong, but only who each of you is. Let the differences stand side by side.

5. <u>Be Accountable</u> for your actions and feelings. You do not need to justify them as right; their value is that they express who you really are. In this way you are learning to be assertive without yourself becoming judgmental and belittling of your spouse.

Each of these responses shows respect both for yourself and for your spouse. You thus become a more responsive person, even if your spouse refuses to grow in his or her responsiveness.

The Decision-Making Process

Conflict between spouses often arises when there are differences of opinion regarding decisions that need to be made. The decision-making process easily turns into a power struggle over whether the decision should go the husband's way or the wife's way. Such decisions easily remain locked in power struggles which one wins and the other must lose. The two spouses will then limit themselves to the kinds of responses to each other that will diminish the relationship rather than enhance it.

The following diagram suggests a three-stage process that can facilitate making decisions and will then enhance the marital relationship. The same process can be adapted to resolving other conflicts in the marriage.

Diagram of a Model for the Decision-Making Process

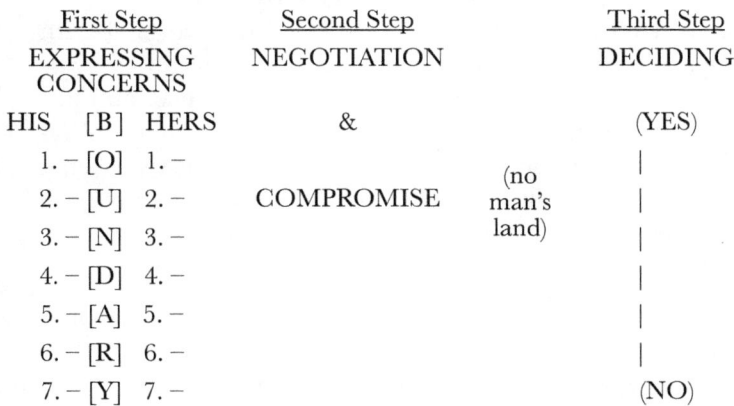

First Step	Second Step		Third Step
EXPRESSING CONCERNS	NEGOTIATION		DECIDING
HIS [B] HERS	&		(YES)
1. – [O] 1. –		(no	|
2. – [U] 2. –	COMPROMISE	man's	|
3. – [N] 3. –		land)	|
4. – [D] 4. –			|
5. – [A] 5. –			|
6. – [R] 6. –			|
7. – [Y] 7. –			(NO)

The diagram indicates three steps in the process of decision making or conflict resolution. In the first stage of the process each spouse has the freedom to identify his and her concerns as one's own, without using them as an argument for a final decision. Each concern has some validity regardless of how the final resolution turns out. The concerns of the husband are best kept separate (the "boundary") from those of the wife. In this way each can acknowledge the value of the other's concerns without prejudice to the outcome. Such validation of each other is the most important part of the process.

> Several years ago my wife and I had differing ideas as to what to do on our two-week summer vacation. We had planned to spend the entire time relaxing at Devil's Lake, Wisconsin—until she decided it was important for the family to visit her aging mother in Minnesota. One of my wife's concerns was that it had been several years since we had gone as a whole family to visit her mother, and her mother had just turned 81. How much longer would she live? And with our children growing up, that year was likely to be the last that we would all be together on a vacation. She felt that we owed it to our children to visit Grandma as a family one more time. We didn't need to spend the whole vacation there—just a few days. We could still go camping part of the time. Each of the concerns she identified was valid. Yet none of them decided the issue.
>
> I also had my legitimate concerns. Working with people as we both do, we've always taken vacations away from friends and relatives so that we can relax and just be together. Our oldest daughter had a summer job at the university and could be with us only for a weekend. Driving 500 miles each way (to Minnesota) would not leave much time for her to enjoy the weekend or for us to have fun with her.

Often what happens in disputes of this kind is that any concerns that are raised by either spouse immediately become an argument for or against the final decision. Neither one is really listening to the concerns of the other. The responses to each other will be largely oppositional, and as a result neither one will feel understood or valued with one's own concerns.

The "no man's land" between the final decision and the rest of the process is essential for breaking up such power struggles.

It means agreeing to set aside arguments over the final decision. Once all the concerns of each spouse are in the open, a process of negotiation and compromise can be pursued (step 2). All the possibilities of combining the concerns of each can be explored through an imaginative "what if…" process. Here, too, the "no man's land" must not be crossed; arguments about the final decision are out of bounds.

> What if we would leave Friday afternoon and return Sunday evening? What if we took two cars so some of us could leave early and one of us could drive up with our daughter later? Or one of us could drive back with her while the others stayed at Grandma's longer. What if we all flew there? Was there any other time that we could visit Grandma as a family?

In step three the YES and NO indicate the initially opposed viewpoints as to the final resolution. A mutual decision will eventually be reached that hopefully incorporates some of the concerns of each spouse (listed in step 1). The "no man's land" will then be crossed together in harmony rather than in opposition. Both spouses will have "won." And the marriage will have won. In following the three-step process each spouse will become increasingly responsive to the other. Each will feel valued and cared for by the other.

> We eventually settled on the idea of going to visit Grandma for a whole week during Christmas vacation (in spite of some hesitation about winter driving). We had a very relaxing summer vacation at Devil's Lake. A few months later, despite sliding off the road once each way, we had a most enjoyable Christmas as a family with Grandma. The concerns of both of us were largely met. This resolution became all the more meaningful to us when we learned, in February, that my wife's mother had terminal cancer. In April we were in Minnesota, once again, for her funeral.

Summary

A Trinitarian model for marriage deserves to replace the traditional hierarchical or authoritarian model. The basic issue in every marriage has to do with respecting the individual characteristics, concerns, and sensitivities of each spouse by the other. In a satisfying and growing marriage, what belongs to the individuality of each spouse will increasingly come to expression throughout the years of the marriage. To whatever extent each spouse experiences this occurring, the sense of unity and mutual bonding between them will at the same time be growing stronger and deeper. Satisfying marriages are relationships that work out a successful interplay between the need for separateness and the need for togetherness in all the key marital areas. A healthy process for conflict resolution and for making decisions is based on these same two principles. Conflict produces growth in a marriage when we move away from a concern with proving who is right and who is wrong, and toward a continuing discovery of who each of us is.

In a marriage which embodies the two principles of respect for each other's individuality and cultivation of marital union, trust is repeatedly experienced, as God intended when he created us in his image. Separateness moves toward new wholeness, as in creation. Then the marriage will image the reality of the one God who is Father, Son, and Holy Spirit–distinct persons who are fully one.

Does the model of the Trinity also assist us in understanding some of the basic dynamics and issues within a growing family composed of parents and children? That is the focus of our attention in the next chapter.

8

LIVING RESPONSIVELY AS
PARENTS IN A FAMILY

Families come in many shapes and sizes. They always have. The two-parent nuclear family with two or three children appears to be a recent phenomenon on the broader screen of history. In other eras and other cultures the extended family was close-knit and more functional than it is today. Some families have had nannies who in effect raised the children. Other families have had multiple wives and mothers. In some families maids and servants were considered part of the broader "household." Just as there is no one form that a marriage must take according to the Scriptures, so there is no one form that is mandated for the family.

Today the two-parent nuclear family is still seen by the majority of people in the Western world as the ideal to be wished for, even if not always attained or sustained. Two other common forms of the family are the single-parent family and the blended family. Some families go through a succession of all three forms, functioning initially as an intact two-parent family, then, after going through a divorce or widowhood, as a single-parent family for a time, and later, through remarriage with another single parent, forming a blended family.

Whatever its form, the family remains the social unit within which most individuals develop a sense of loyalty and bonding with other individuals. Within the family the responsive capacity with which we are all created comes to its first expression, and here it is exercised and developed. It is here that children learn ways of responding that will enhance their continued growth in responsivity.

But they may also develop patterns that obstruct the development of their capacity to be responsive. To build a family in a world already redeemed by God, what guidelines can parents follow that will facilitate rather than restrict the development of responsiveness in and among all family members?

The Trinitarian Model

All of us develop some notion of what a family is or what it should be. As we build our own family, we consciously or unconsciously make use of some model that guides us in our attempt to form a happy family life for ourselves as parents and children. However vague or well-defined that model is, we keep coming back to it from time to time as we try to figure out how to deal with the issues present at a particular stage of family life. Whatever model we make use of will reflect the values that operate in our lives; at the same time, as we make use of a particular model, it will in turn reinforce those values.

Perhaps we use an economic model, derived from the hopes and dreams of being a success in our American culture. We want our family to live in the suburbs in a single-family home with a two-stall garage for our two cars, and we want our children to do at least as well as or better than we have done economically. If we are moving toward that goal we feel that we are doing well in raising our family; if not, we are not doing so well.

Most of us use our family of origin as a model for managing our own growing family. In some ways we do that deliberately; in other ways we may do it without being aware of it at all. For some of us that may involve still using a hierarchical or authoritarian model for raising children, much like our parents used in both their marital relationship and in raising us. Following this model, the child's role is to learn respect and obedience, and the parents' task is to make sure that the children are obedient and respectful. How well everyone fulfills these roles is what determines how well the family is functioning.

Virginia Satir, an early leader in the family systems movement, suggested that the hanging mobile, often placed above an infant's crib, can serve as a helpful analogy for family life. A mobile has a number of different objects hanging from it, but they are all suspended from a common connection. The mobile will find a stable balance when undisturbed, but, once disturbed–by whatever cause–each piece will begin to move. Each individual object on the mobile will influence the movement of every other object, but each piece will itself also be affected by the motion of every other piece. In family life the mobile analogy can help us overcome the tendency to deal with family problems by blaming only one family member while ignoring what we ourselves, or other family members, contribute by our own reactions.

Satir's analogy of the mobile reminds me of the Christian doctrine of the Trinity. The mobile has a number of distinct, individual pieces, each with its own characteristics of size, shape, and weight, which nonetheless form a unity. The Trinity has three distinct persons who form one God. And that suggests to me that the Trinity can serve us well as a model not only for marriage, but also for family life.

The doctrine of the Trinity contains two basic principles: first is the distinctness of the persons without any confusion or any subordination; second is the unity or oneness of the godhead. Since we are created in God's image it is no surprise to find that the same two principles form the basis of healthy family life. First is the principle that each person in the family, including each child, is to be treated as a distinct person in his or her own right. Second is the principle that a sense of bonding or unity needs to be cultivated among the family members. As we live out of these two principles, family relationships will promote the growth of responsivity in and among all family members. Violation of either of these two principles will hinder such development.

Everything else that can be said about healthy family living is simply an unfolding of these two basic principles. The problems that we encounter in family living are all expressions of the tension and the mystery that we experience in trying to embrace both of these principles at the same time. How are we to encourage our children to "be your own person" and to "do your own thing" while at the same time enabling them to value family togetherness and loyalty, as well as loyalty to church, to community, to nation, and, indeed, to all humankind?

Deliberate Parenting vs. Parenting by Instinct

Using the Trinity as a model for dealing with the issues of family life requires more than relying on our own instincts as parents. It calls for examining the unconscious models that we all do use. That enables us to develop a deliberate plan and rationale for what we are trying to accomplish as parents.

As we go through the years of parenting, each of us develops our own ways of responding to our children. Many of these ways appear to be an instinctive part of us. We may like the ways that we respond, or we may berate ourselves for them, but our responses seem, in either case, to be a natural part of ourselves. We may feel guilty when we yell at the kids, but what can you expect, we ask, when they are so obstinate and you've told them umpteen times already to do something? For the most part, we do our parenting "by instinct."

When we react to a family problem under stress, we also instinctively draw on our experience as children with our own parents. Without being fully aware of it, we often react to our children much as our parents reacted to us, and it may seem unquestioningly right for us to do so. The other parent, of course, will probably be doing the same thing. The two of you are each using a different model with which you are familiar from long experience in your own family of origin. Herein lies the source of many of the conflicts that arise between parents as they discipline their children. It is also the source of many of the dysfunctional family patterns that are handed on from one generation to the next, often to "the third and the fourth generation," and sometimes beyond.

When we rely on instinct alone in parenting, the range of responses that we develop will be very limited. In many cases the primary responses will be negative ones, especially if that is what we experienced in our own childhood. Most of our energy will be invested in blaming and in trying to control our children. As a result we, in turn, teach our children the same limited range of responses for dealing with frustrating circumstances.

The more deliberately we as parents reflect on what we are trying to accomplish, the more likely we are to enlarge our own capacity to respond constructively to our children. At the same time we will enable them to be enhancing their responsive capacities to meet life's challenges and to develop meaningful relationships.

Let's look at some of the recurring issues that arise as we draw on the Trinitarian model for parenting and family life.

Equality vs. Subordination

Are we as parents to relate to our children as though they are our equals? Or do we assume that they are our subordinates? These questions cannot be answered with a simple yes or no. Yet how we do respond to such questions may affect to a considerable degree how we relate to our children. In opposition to an authoritarian model, many experts today consider the family a democratic institution in which all family members have an equal say in any decisions that concern the whole family.

As an antidote to abusive parental tyranny that has existed in many families, the democratic model of equality is appealing and desirable. Children of any age have a right to be treated as persons to whom is due the same respect and dignity that we claim for ourselves as parents. Nor should the needs of children be subordinated to the needs of the adults in the family; in some sense the needs of the children should supersede those of the parents since children are less able to meet their own needs. However, if a focus on democracy and equality leads parents to fear saying no to their children, to hesitate to set the limits that children need, and to avoid teaching moral and religious values, then it seems doubtful that healthy family life will develop. Children are not given a legal right to vote, to drink alcohol, or to smoke, even in a democracy; even in a democracy they, though persons, are not given free rein to do as they please. Children are children. They are not adults.

The key issue here is that a child is to be looked upon and treated as a fully distinct person in his or her own right. As a person, the child possesses fully as much worth and value as the adult who cares for her or him. In this regard we dare not look at a child as in any way "subordinate" to the father or the mother. The child is not an extension of the parent. The little boy does not exist to live out the unfulfilled dreams of his father. The little girl does not have as her mission in life to give her mother a sense of accomplishment. Whatever the father's dreams are for himself, fulfilled or not, and whatever the mother may need in order to experience success, the little boy and the little girl, as distinct persons, are entitled to develop their own dreams and to discover for themselves what brings them satisfaction. The child does not exist for the sake of the parent.

Nor do parents need to live only for the sake of their children. A father's existence is not defined solely by his being a father and breadwinner. He has many other dimensions to his life. And a mother's existence is also not defined by her being a mother, housewife, and perhaps breadwinner. She, too, has other dimensions to herself that add shape and substance to her life.

In the same way, however, a child's existence is not defined solely be being a child. Johnny is the unique child that he is, with the particular personality traits that he has developed to the age he now is. He has his own kind of needs, which may differ from those of his sister Susie. And Susie's life is not defined only by her being a child or by her being a girl. She has her own developmental age and her own individual personality traits, as well as her own interests and needs that enable her and us to discover who she is as a person.

Following in the Trinitarian principle of the distinctness of persons, we will strive to respect and treat each person in the family as the particular person he or she is. We will value the personality of each one. We will respect the sexuality of each family member and his or her right to privacy. We will not try to make one child be like another. We will take into account the particular age of each family member, treating adults as the adults they are, and the children as the children they are. We will see that when each family member is treated as a distinct person, questions regarding equality versus subordination disappear.

Objectives vs. Expectations

If we are to honor the distinctness of each person in the family, it is helpful to distinguish our parental objectives from the expectations we have of our children at any particular age. Parents sometimes confuse these two, ignoring the significant difference between them. Objectives have to do with what we are raising our children to become when they eventually reach maturity or adulthood. Sometimes we have hidden agendas or objectives for them that we do not make clear even to ourselves, much less to them. As parents we will legitimately have our own objectives in raising our children, and these will be determined, to some degree, by our social, moral, and religious values. But we do well, in any case, to deliberately examine our objectives and to test their validity. At a minimum, most of us will have as an objective that our children will become reasonably responsible and independent, able to take care of and support themselves by the time they reach young adulthood. Difficulties arise when such laudable objectives are confused with current expectations.

Expectations have to do with what we assume a child is capable of doing *at the age* he or she now is. A two-year-old cannot be expected to function as a ten-year-old, nor is a fourteen-year-old yet ready to function as a 21-year-old. It can be a difficult task for parents to determine just what are reasonable expectations for any particular age, and for their own individual children. To enhance their own capacity for responding to their children they may need to work at becoming familiar, through print or online resources, with the various stages of childhood and adolescent development, and perhaps even attend a workshop on parenting skills.

What sometimes happens, especially in the early teenage years, is that parents focus on how important it is for their children to "be responsible." The parents become frustrated when the child or adolescent shows any sign of being "irresponsible." They begin to berate the child and perhaps punish her or him. In many instances they are confusing what are reasonable *objectives for the future* with unreasonable *expectations for the present*. I have often witnessed parents' attempts to reason and even argue with a sullen adolescent, trying to convince the teenager that the limits or rules that the parents have set really are quite reasonable, and that the teenager should not be upset by them. When the adolescent remains unconvinced or still angry, the parent, in turn, becomes angry. It is at that point that the parent needs to be reminded that it is not reasonable to expect the fourteen-year-old to think and feel and react like a forty-year-old. (And then the parent also needs to be reminded that it is not appropriate for an adult to respond on the level of the adolescent, which we do easily enough.)

Many power struggles with adolescents could be avoided if parents would respect the fact that teenagers are not adults. They can be expected to react as adolescents and not as adults. That doesn't mean giving them everything they may want or demand.

But it does mean respecting that they have their own ideas, tastes, feelings, and reactions as adolescents, which we cannot expect to be the same as our own adult reactions and feelings.

It is fully understandable that parents of adolescents long for the day when their offspring will function as responsible adults. But when we as parents confuse objectives for the future with current expectations, we are treating our children as though they exist to meet our needs. We then limit our own growth in responsiveness toward them as the distinct persons they are. To that extent we also impede the development of their responsivity.

Respect vs. Demands

Another legitimate objective that most parents have for their children is that they learn to show respect. Children need to learn respect for their parents, for their teachers, and for others in positions of authority. They need to learn respect for their playmates and other peers. They need to learn respect for all other human beings and for all forms of life. They need to learn respect for themselves as well. But how do parents effectively teach respect to their children?

An infant has no concept of respect–hungry at 2:00 a.m., she has no respect for her mother's tiredness and need for sleep. The two-year-old child who sets his mind against picking up his toys is not showing respect for the parent, though he seems to be responding quite normally for his age. Similarly, a fourteen-year-old who explodes in anger when told that he is not allowed to stay out with his friends until 1:00 a.m. may not be acting respectfully at the moment, but he may be expressing himself appropriately for his age.

In each instance the parents' objective remains the same: to teach the child how to show respect. But what can be realistically expected of the child will vary both with the child's age and with his or her level of emotional development and maturity. Even a relatively mature adolescent under stress reverts back to the kind of childhood outburst that seems to show little respect at the moment. How are parents to react?

It is tempting for parents to respond by demanding respect on the spot. Such a demand allows little room for any spontaneous expression of emotion on the child's or the teenager's part. If, when a teenage daughter responds to limits with an angry outburst and Dad demands that she apologize and show respect, she may, instead, become more defiant, escalating the power struggle, or she may become moody, withdrawn, and depressed, conforming out of fear and thereby appearing to show respect, but in reality simply shutting down her feelings. Neither leads to a healthy outcome.

When a parent's response is limited to one of seeking "respect on demand," two results often follow. First, the parent's own responsive capacity in relation to the child will become self-limiting instead of a source of growth for the parent. And second, the child's reaction will become either aggressive or defensive, either of which limits the child's growth in responsivity. This is the source of many of the power struggles that escalate through the adolescent years of family life.

Parents will not succeed in teaching genuine respect by demanding it, nor by blaming, condemning, or punishing, nor by lecturing (invariably condescending). All of those measures attempt to resolve the issue all at once. We would do better, however, to look at teaching respect as an eighteen (or more) year process. The key to the process lies in the responsiveness that parents themselves show toward the child or adolescent throughout these years.

There are two ingredients in this responsiveness that are essential for successfully helping children to learn respect. The first ingredient is that of showing respect for the child or teenager. Children learn the meaning and value of respect when they experience their parents treating them with respect. That may not always be easy for a parent to do, but, recognizing that it is even more difficult for a child or adolescent to be respectful when upset, the parent can be firm in saying no to an unacceptable demand while still respecting the child's angry reaction to that "no."

The second ingredient is the parent's respect for his or her own needs and feelings. A parent can communicate to the child that he has respect for his own limits, and that he feels comfortable with them. For example, I may say "no" to my sixteen-year-old daughter's request to drive a carload of young people for the church youth group outing. "But I'm a good driver!" she protests. I can agree with her on that, but simply explain to her that, in view of her still-limited driving experience, I do not want to spend the whole evening worrying. I respect my own feelings. When children experience Dad and Mom respecting their own needs and feelings, the children learn the meaning of respect.

Parents set the tone for family living by demonstrating respect for the needs and feelings of both their children and themselves. The children will then learn, however gradually, the value of respect in human relationships. Displaying respect for others, an essential ingredient in all relationships of friendship and intimacy, is one of the most important ways for us to enhance our capacity to be responsive to others.

Trust vs. Authority/Obedience

But we still have questions. Is not one of the most important issues for children that they learn obedience? Above all else, do not children need to learn how to respect authority? Don't they need parents to be teaching them this obedience? If they do not learn obedience, is not everything else lost? After all, even Jesus needed to learn obedience both to his earthly parents (Luke 2:51) and to his heavenly Father through the things that he suffered (Heb. 5:8). And Paul writes, "Children, obey your parents in the Lord, for this is right" (Eph. 6:1). If children need to learn obedience, is it not especially important in an age of permissiveness that parents exercise their parental authority with confidence?

The answer is that all of the above is, of course, true. Children do need to learn obedience, and parents do need to be able at times to take charge with confident authority. Children need parents to set limits for them and give direction. A child who never learns to obey will be a child who becomes totally self-centered and who, as an adult, will know little about how to form relationships of intimacy. In learning obedience, a child is learning how to blend his own individual will in with that of others. He is learning, in other words, that his will is not, after all, the only and ultimate measure of all that is good and right. Obedience can be considered the antidote to the original sin and all other sin.

Obedience is not, however, something that parents need from the child for their own sake. In Ephesians 6 when Paul calls children to obey their parents he does not, in turn, call on parents to cultivate the power to make their children obey. What corresponds on the parents' side is rather the admonition not to provoke the children to anger, but to bring them up. To lift up and not to put down—that is the parents' role. Parents do not need authority for their own sake, but for the purpose of helping the children grow up to responsive adulthood. Children do not need to obey for the sake of their parents, but for their own growth and development.

Obedience alone, however, especially when imposed by a heavy-handed authority, will not result in a healthy family life. Obedience, important as it may be, is not the main issue. *Grace* is the main issue. Grace invites trust; grace also restores broken trust. A parent's primary task is to create an atmosphere of grace where trust can flourish and grow. In such an atmosphere, responsiveness of children to parents and to each other will develop right along with a growing responsiveness on the part of parents to the children and their ever-changing needs. The more such trust permeates the relationships within a family, the less emphasis there will be on authority/obedience for its own sake.

The single most important gift that parents can give to their children, especially to their teenagers, is their trust. Yes, parents really do need to trust their adolescent children. And teenagers really do need to experience the trust—unconditional trust—that their parents have in them. Unconditional trust does not mean being naïve or overly optimistic or blindly confident. It does not involve saying, "My child would never do such a thing!" There could be many things which experience has taught us that we cannot trust one of our teenagers never to do. Even then, we need not make a global assault on an adolescent's character by calling her or him "untrustworthy."

Trust means being able to "count on" someone for a specific behavior. A teenager who lies cannot be counted on to tell the truth. One who repeatedly breaks curfew cannot be trusted to come home on time. No teenager can be trusted never to make mistakes. How then can we possibly trust our adolescents unconditionally?

What we can trust is that they are worthwhile kids even when they do make mistakes, sometimes costly mistakes. We can trust that they will turn out all right and will live worthwhile lives. We can trust because we live in a world already redeemed by God, and God has promised to be their God as well as ours. That is his promise in baptism. Our children need us to live by faith in that promise. We really can trust that they will turn out OK! When we do, they learn to trust the promise, too, and thereby learn to trust themselves.

Enjoyment vs. Frustration

Anyone who has been a parent for long knows that frustration comes with the territory. Parents of teenagers, especially, know the meaning of frustration! Frustration, however, means that you care. Coming from the caring heart of a parent, it means that you want something good, something better than what is happening at the moment, for your child and for his or her future. Frustration therefore is a normal part of parenting and does not represent something wrong with the parent.

By accepting frustration as a normal part of dealing with the legitimate immaturity of our children we can learn to focus on the fun and youthful sparkle that they bring into our lives. Children of any age need to experience their parents' enjoyment of them as their children. They need to sense the delight which their parents feel in relating to them as their own offspring. When that sense of delight and enjoyment is missing, something vital is lost in the soul of the child, something that obstructs his or her own capacity for enjoyment. In one form or another every child needs to hear the message, "You are my child, and I take delight in you!"

Even Jesus needed to hear that message. Both at his baptism (Matt. 3:17) and again on the Mount of Transfiguration (Matt. 17:5) he heard, "This is my beloved son, in whom I am well pleased." "You are my child, and I take delight in you." Is it any surprise that a son who hears this message again and again actually takes delight in freely doing such a father's will?

Discipline vs. Punishment

No child ever needs to be punished. Punishment has to do with retribution that is due for wrong. Christ has already atoned for the sin of the world; additional punishment is no longer needed. To punish a child is to reject Christ's atonement. What children need is discipline, as Christian psychologist Dr. Bruce Narramore has pointed out (*No Condemnation: Rethinking Guilt Motivation in Counseling, Preaching, and Parenting,* 2002).

In dealing with the discipline of children, two basic but related questions arise: How can parents best respond to the misbehavior of their children? What rationale for responding to their children's behavior will best guide their parenting?

Both of these questions—and not just the first—draw out the responsiveness of parents. Answers come from any number of authors and agencies: Bill Gothard, James Dobson, Rudolf Dreikurs, "Active Parenting," "P.E.T." (Parent Effectiveness Training), the Adler Institute, the Family Institute of Chicago, and many others—all have their own theory and practice for good parenting. Most of these are worth checking out. But in the end, parents will respond to what makes sense to them, and will implement only what they themselves are ready to follow through on. What is more, only those parents who are seeking to expand their ways of responding to their children are likely to pay much attention to any discussion on parenting.

Each of us as parents is responsive to our children. We cannot *not* be responsive unless we are already dead. What we are dealing with in disciplining children is the reality that some parental responses are likely to limit or hurt our children's growth, and our own growth as parents, as well, whereas other responses are more likely to enhance growth—for children and parents alike. This perspective requires that parents keep a clear distinction between what the child may be doing wrong and what the parent is doing in response.

Parents can easily fall into the trap of automatically justifying their response by pronouncing that what the child has done is wrong. But no matter what wrong the child has done, parents still have a wide variety of responses to choose from. Some of those responses will enable the child to grow; other responses will more likely stifle growth, and may even do great damage. The objective of discipline is not to control and thus limit the child's responses, but to discourage those responses in the child that are hurtful and self-limiting rather than growth enhancing. Unlike punishment, discipline is always geared toward the child's growth. Discipline opens new avenues for the child to respond to others, and to all of life, in expanding ways.

Parental responses that involve blaming, ridiculing the child, withdrawal from the child, or merely controlling the child, may meet some need in the parent but will limit rather than promote the child's growth. Such responses will likewise limit the parent's own capacity to be responsive to the child's needs.

Discipline is a problem-solving process. The parent's role is to identify the child's problem as a recurring one, and the resolution as a helpful one. The challenge is then to find what disciplinary means will help the child reach the desired solution. Handled in this way, discipline promotes both the child's and the family's growth. Discipline provides the context for both the child and the parents to grow in their responsiveness toward each other, and then toward others.

Building Self-Esteem and Family Unity

Everything we have been discussing under the heading of "Deliberate Parenting" is what goes into building a child's self-esteem. A child learns how to value herself from the way she experiences her parents treating and valuing her. A child inherently trusts and believes the parent–for better or for worse.

A parent who treats a child as if she has inferior worth, who puts expectations on her that she cannot possibly attain, who puts her down with disdain and contempt, who communicates to her that she will never amount to anything, who displays primarily frustration with her, who repeatedly punishes her as if she were inherently a bad person, teaches this child to treat herself in the same way. Throughout her life such a child will doubt her own worth. She will be quick to put herself down and discount her achievements, no matter how excellent they are. She will likely become anxious or depressed, or both. She will find ways to unconsciously punish herself, for example, by sabotaging her own success and her relationships with others.

Low self-esteem is not a passive "disease." It is an active way of treating oneself badly. All of us have elements or times of low self-esteem, but where the problem is severe and persistent, its origin often lies in a parent's way of treating the child. The child inherently trusts the parent's way, and therefore imitates it as the only conceivable way to treat oneself.

But what happens if a parent treats a child from the outset as a distinct person of equal worth with him- or herself? What if this parent encourages the child with realistic and attainable expectations, and treats his feelings, ideas, needs, and sensitivities with respect? Suppose this parent also communicates a basic sense of trust in the child even when he makes mistakes, and displays a sense of delight and enjoyment in the child in an ongoing way. Suppose this parent, with some consistency, employs discipline where necessary that is clearly identified as a means toward helping the child grow in his ability to relate to others. Then this child will learn to treat himself throughout his adult life in the same way: as a worthwhile person who is capable of growth even when he faces frustration and failure. He will trust his own feelings and ideas, and will value his own sensitivities. He will know how to enjoy himself and will find pleasure in others as well. He will have a firm foundation for building meaningful relationships that endure. He will have learned to respond to himself and to all of life in ways that continually open up new possibilities for him. He will understand the religious meaning of grace, for he will have experienced it throughout his growing up, even if he never once heard the word.

What we particularly need to note here is that all of those ingredients that go into building a positive sense of self-esteem and independence in children are the very same ingredients that go into building a solid and growing sense of family unity. When children experience parents treating them as worthwhile persons in their own right and encouraging them to think well of themselves as separate, independent persons, these children are going to value that support and value all the persons in the family who are a part of it. Here family togetherness and loyalty will not be formed out of fear and held together by parental inducements of guilt, but will be free and voluntary, which makes this unity all the more precious to those who experience it.

Dysfunctional and Functional Families

But not all families experience a healthy unity. Families become "disengaged" when the individual members each go their own way, with no real sense of bonding. That occurs when the resources for developing self-esteem are not found within the family but can only be sought and discovered outside the family. Family unity then disintegrates, and something valuable is lost.

Families become "enmeshed" when everyone in the family is subtly or blatantly coerced into thinking, feeling, and acting in the same way. Individual family members are discouraged from expressing their own feelings, ideas, or ambitions. Family unity may then prevail on the surface; a united front may be presented to the outside world; below the surface, however, resentments, hurts, and self-doubts continually stir. In this case, too, the family is not a source of self-esteem for individual family members, but is germinating problems that will emerge in the future.

In what today are called "dysfunctional" families we usually discover elements of either disengagement or enmeshment. To some extent, all families have dysfunctional elements. No one has ever grown up in a perfect family. One of my favorite cartoons is that of a large convention hall, with a long banner strung above the entryway: ANNUAL ACONP CONVENTION. In the huge auditorium only two isolated individuals are present; it's the annual convention for "Adult Children of Normal Parents."

What nonetheless characterizes severely dysfunctional families and makes them different from functional families is the lack of most of those ingredients that both build individual self-esteem and also create a free and voluntary sense of family unity. In such families the usual messages, often more non-verbal than verbal, are: Don't think! Don't feel! Don't talk! And above all, Don't trust! Children are discouraged from thinking for themselves, are given messages that treat their feelings as either unimportant or as bad, and are not allowed to comment on what is actually occurring within the family—much less talk to "outsiders" about it. Family secrets are common in such families. Rather than being nurtured and built up, trust is constantly broken.

Dysfunctional families are produced where alcoholism or some other addiction is present and its impact denied, resulting in behaviors that are either abusive or simply neglectful. Even without alcoholism or any other overt addiction, where ongoing physical abuse, emotional abuse, or sexual abuse occurs, the growing family will become dysfunctional. Such a family cannot achieve a balance between the growth of individual self-esteem and the development of healthy family unity. An unhealthy emotional dependency on the family develops, which finds its source in fear and inadequacy rather than in trust and encouragement. This is the family that is likely to produce adults who struggle all their lives with anxiety, depression, and disturbed relationships.

Reasonably functional families are those that pursue a course that enables children to emerge into adulthood with enough self-confidence to build healthy and mature relationships with friends, in marriage and family, and in church and society. Such relationships will promote individual growth and meaningful bonding at the same time.

Adult Children and Their Parents

Young children and adolescents are not the only ones who go through stages in their lives. As children emerge into independent adulthood, the relationship with their parents changes significantly even while it continues to be a powerful one—again, for better or for worse. As we move through the adult years of our lives, we all go through many stages: from being a young adult attempting to establish oneself in the adult world, to being in mid-stride as we build a family and begin to feel settled in the workplace, to going through the middle-life awareness of aging and adjusting to the "empty nest," to reaching retirement, and eventually facing all the issues of old age and dying. Only when death comes does the process of going through stages cease—at least as far as we can now see.

Families, and not just individuals, also go through stages. A family starts out in the family formation stage, begun with dating and established in the early years of the marriage. Next comes the family building stage, as children are born, and much of the focus and energy revolves around making provisions for the growing family. As the children move into the teenage years, the tasks of the family begin to shift from family building to preparing the adolescents for independent living. The family is then in the "launching" stage. And eventually, as the children all move out, the family reaches the "empty nest" stage.

Transitions

Many family problems arise in the transition from one stage of family life to another. In transition periods we gradually let go of what we valued in the preceding stage and take hold of what the new stage has to offer. If we hang on too long to what was good in the earlier stage while not embracing what belongs to the new stage, tensions in family life will arise. For example, the husband who, after marriage, continues to go out with "the boys" several nights a week while his new wife sits home alone is failing to let go of the past stage and embrace what belongs to the new stage. Again, the transition from the family building stage of family life to the adolescent stage finds some parents upset that their sweet little children are now beginning to pull away and prefer to be with friends. Later, the transition from adolescence to young adulthood, and then from the family launching stage to the empty nest stage, are also navigated with great difficulty by many families.

The new realities of an emerging stage call for new responses from those who enter it. The list of books on parents and infants, on parents and growing children, and on parents and adolescents is long. But few books focus on the relationship between parents and the children who have become adults. No relationship has received less attention than this, yet a goodly number of the issues for which young and middle-aged adults enter therapy involve ongoing tension with parents. These tensions with parents will reproduce themselves in the relationships with one's spouse and one's own children, and others as well.

As the children enter into adulthood, parents can finally relax a bit. The load of responsibility which weighs on them as their children are growing up and going through adolescence is now eased. This can be a time to enjoy their adult children as they see them taking on adult responsibilities such as beginning a job or career, entering into marriage, beginning to build a family of their own as grandchildren are born. Young adults can also finally begin to relax with their parents as they get to know them as real persons rather than as authority figures who restrict privileges and dispense disapproval.

The difficulty in making this transition is equally present on both sides of the relationship. Parents who have invested a great deal of themselves in their children may have a hard time letting go of the responsibility for and control over their offspring. There are times when health problems can result in a parent's becoming dependent on adult children. More often, though, a parent can become emotionally dependent on the child, needing to think of the adult child as still needing parental guidance. A mother whose whole life and sense of purpose has revolved around her children may have a hard time letting go of what gave her life meaning, leading her to treat them as still dependent on her. She may become subtly or not-so-subtly controlling; she may make guilt-inducing comments that manipulate an adult child into doing her bidding. A father who for years has derived a sense of fulfillment from providing for his children may insist on buying a car or even a house for the adult child, thereby keeping him or her emotionally indebted to him. Parents can continue to see their role as that of giving unsolicited guidance through comments and critiques of the way their adult children deal with their children, their jobs, or their life-style.

The adult child will often contribute to this process by giving in to it, by rebelling against it through angry retorts or disguised resistance, or by avoiding the parents as much as possible. All of these responses to continuing parental control portray a young adult who still feels and reacts as an adolescent under the power of the parent. They are not yet the responses of an adult who is ready to claim full adulthood by developing new responses appropriate to an adult status. Adults in their twenties, thirties, and beyond often say something like this: "I wish my parents would just respect the fact that I'm an adult now and can make my own decisions and have my own life!" But if such an adult still needs permission and approval from the parents to think and act as an adult, it is evident that he or she has not yet made the transition to full adulthood. For many individuals that transition is not completed until one is well into the thirties and forties. Sometimes it is never successfully made at all.

Claiming Adulthood

To claim one's own adulthood, the adult child needs to develop new responses to his or her parent which respect the distinctness of persons who, as parent and child, are both adult. Adult children often continue fighting, literally, for the parents' approval. It is as if the validity of their own choices depends on that approval. They cannot feel confident in their decisions when these differ from Dad's, or do not receive Mom's okay. If Dad or Mom is upset, disapproving, or attempting to control the decision, the adult child feels an impulse either to comply or to fight back, or to sulk and withdraw.

At this stage of family relationships, respecting and honoring parents means experiencing them and responding to them as the specific persons they are. Disapproval expressed by a parent no longer tells an adult child who she or he is, whether good or bad, as it did throughout childhood. Back then a parent's disapproval was a clear message to the child about the child. Now that the child is an adult, the parent's disapproval can be respected and honored as a disclosure not about the child but about the parent.

For instance, Dad criticizes the house his son buys because of its open design which will probably involve higher heating bills. The son may react defensively, pointing out all the virtues of the house in order to persuade Dad to give his approval. The assumption here is that the son really does need his father's approval; he cannot allow his father to have his own values as the distinct person that he is. Yet it would be quite possible to respond by expressing respect for the values and opinions of the parent. Listening to criticism by the parent of the adult child is one way in which the child can come to know the parent as the distinct person he is. Dad's criticism of the house may reflect the value he has always placed on conserving fuel and being thrifty, values that were forged through the difficult years of raising a family during the depression era. The more an adult child can let go of the need to win the parent's approval, the more he or she will come to know the parent in a new light. The relationship will then become more open, more free, and more enjoyable on both sides. As the adult child increasingly claims his or her adulthood, the chances are that critical parents will also increasingly come to respect that adulthood, and will then be more likely to let go of the need to maintain control over their adult children.

The key to a healthy relationship between adult children and their parents lies in a mutual respect for the distinctness of each person as the individual he or she is. Communicating such respect is at the same time the key to a new and deepening adult relationship between parents and their grown children. When this new phase of the relationship is working well, the parents are able to be supportive and responsive to their children as adults, and these newly adult children are in turn more fully able than before to appreciate and be responsive to their parents as the individual persons they are.

Summary

The original drama of creation plays itself out once again, now in the arena of family life. By maintaining and highlighting the separateness or distinctness of each family member, the identity of each individual is enhanced while at the same time a new whole, the family unit, is formed—a unit that is of inestimable value. Not even sin can totally destroy the working of this process, for we live in a world already redeemed by God.

Parenting requires more than just reacting out of the instincts that were formed through our own experiences in childhood. As we develop a deliberate plan for parenting, using the Trinity as our model, we will treat each person in the family with the same respect we want for ourselves, taking into account the age, personality, gender, and maturity of each one. We will distinguish the objectives we have in raising our children to adulthood from the expectations we have for them at any particular age. We will teach respect by example rather than by demand, and we will maintain a sense of trust in the worth of our children that even their misbehavior cannot undo. Despite frustrations, we will find ways to enjoy and show delight in our children. Discipline will be carried out to promote continuing growth in responsive living rather than merely to punish misbehavior. As we follow the principles derived from a Trinitarian model for family life, both individual self-esteem and family unity will develop together through the stages of family life. The same principles apply to the new relationship that develops with parents as children reach adulthood. At every stage of family life respect for the distinctness of each individual family member is what generates wholeness and unity within the family.

In a redeemed world, however, renewed wholeness goes beyond the family. In the church we see the formation of a broader wholeness called forth by the redemptive work of Christ and his Spirit. This is the discussion we seek to undertake in chapter 9.

9

LIVING RESPONSIVELY
as the **BODY OF CHRIST**

The church, like marriage and the family, has come to exist in a wide variety of forms. The range extends from the highly developed ritualism of Eastern Orthodoxy, the sacramentalism of Roman Catholicism, the stately dignity of Episcopalianism, and the intellectualism of Presbyterians and Lutherans, to the simple piety found in an endless variety of independent, charismatic, and fundamentalist churches.

Had this variety come from a healthy growth of diversity springing up among human beings in various cultures we could celebrate it and thank God for it. The reality, however, is that most of the divergences arose from a continuing process of hostile splintering. The divisiveness has often involved bitterness and acrimony, with condemnation of other Christians by those who separated from them. Many of the divisions have broken apart communities and families. Sometimes they have come with ostracism and banishment, with excommunications and inquisitions culminating in burnings at the stake. They have produced lasting pain, with wounds that never quite heal. The many separations have seldom led to the forming of a new and greater wholeness that enriches both parts.

Just as we have often heard warnings of the breakdown and end of the traditional marriage and family, so we continually hear of the coming demise of the church as a significant institution in our modern or post-modern world. Yet with all this, the church goes on. She continues to be a source of both consolation and strength to many. She remains a beacon of hope and a source of social cohesiveness. To our surprise, in the last century she survived seventy years of suppression under atheism in communist Russia and throughout the former Soviet Union.

In a changing and troubled world and in the awareness of her own brokenness, the church still seeks to articulate a sense of her own identity. We now address the question: What does it mean for the church, as the Body of Christ, to live responsively in a broken world redeemed by a sovereign God? What model serves us best in expressing the essence of the church's calling?

The Trinitarian Model

The church will invariably adopt some model after which it will pattern its own existence. As with the family and with marriage, a number of models may be serving at the same time to tell us what the church really is or should be like.

One powerful model that the church consciously adopted early in its history is that of the state. The church came into being when the Roman Empire was still near its peak in power and influence. At the hands of that empire the church suffered repeated periods of persecution that threatened her very existence. But the church itself gradually grew in influence and made peace with the Roman Empire through the conversion of Emperor Constantine in the third century A.D. The church then began to model its own structure after that of the Roman Empire. The structure of the church became increasingly hierarchical. The focus on its own power gradually increased, and through the Middle Ages the church called itself the "Holy Roman Empire"—and acted like an empire. With the emergence of the Renaissance, the Protestant Reformation, and democracy, the empire model has broken down. Even the Roman Church retains only a remnant of imperial trappings.

Today where the church imitates the state, the free-enterprise/ democratic state is the model. It is doubtful whether the state in any form is an adequate model for enabling the church to understand its identity as the Body of Christ in the world. In modeling itself after the state, does the church enhance its responsiveness to God, to its members within, and to the world around it? Or does such a model narrow the church's vision and restrict her capacity to respond to her own members and to the world?

In our contemporary world the church chooses new models to emulate. Some churches appear to be using the entertainment industry as a model for what the church should be if it is to attract an audience and be relevant in the modern world. Pastors become entertainers. They need to create a new "experience" each week in order to draw people to their church.

Other churches look to the business model developed in capitalist countries in the last century. (Not that churches have yet listed themselves on the New York Stock Exchange as a way of gaining capital, but who knows—that may yet come!) Some churches have been looking at the successful business methods that have enabled companies to grow into large, expanding corporations; churches have begun to apply those same methods to their life and growth. These churches, like businesses, are now concerned with goals which must be measurable and attainable to be valid. "Management by objectives" turns ministers into entrepreneurs. Numerical growth, with specific numerical goals to be met within a specific time frame, then becomes the objective.

By following models that are not wrong in themselves but are foreign to its own inner nature, the church easily loses its distinctive character. The more seriously the church today looks to either the entertainment industry or the business world for a model of what the church should be, the more these models will serve in the long run to restrict the church's capacity to be responsive. The church does not exist to entertain people. Nor is the church called by God to build itself up into a successful business. Some immediate benefits may accrue to the church from following these models, but in the long run the more it patterns itself after them the more the church will lose something of its own unique identity, as surely as it did in patterning itself after the Roman Empire. Adding "Holy" to Empire or to Entertainment or to Business does not clarify the identity and calling of the church as the Body of Christ.

The model of the Trinity served us well in helping us to identify many of the basic issues we face both in marriage and in the family as we live responsively with each other. That same model can serve well in helping us to appreciate the unique nature of the church. The two principles derived from the Trinity that we applied to marriage and to family life can be applied equally well to the church. The first is respect for the distinctness of each part or member. The second is concern for the unity of the whole.

The church as a whole—but also any particular denomination, congregation, or individual Christian—will most nearly express its calling as the Body of Christ as it embodies these two principles. The renewed responsiveness that characterizes the casting out of fear and the renewal of faith will grow as each individual member, congregation, and denomination is valued in its uniqueness, while the unity of all these varied parts is at the same time earnestly sought.

The same principles can be seen in other images or metaphors as well, such as the metaphor that Paul applies to the church in I Corinthians 12 where he compares the church to a body which has many distinct parts, each with its own unique function. Each part needs to be valued for what it is, says Paul, but in such a way that the unity of the whole is also promoted. The unity of the whole is recognized in a way that does not diminish but enhances the value of the parts.

Outside the boundaries of these two principles the church's responsivity will diminish. When one part of the church so focuses on itself that it has little regard for the larger body of the church, that part becomes disengaged from the whole and thus dysfunctional. It ceases to be responsive to the other parts and to the whole. But when the larger church suppresses the traits of a smaller part by enforcing conformity, the resulting enmeshment will also block the growth of responsivity. Much of the brokenness of the church involves a loss of responsiveness due to disengagement or enmeshment. All the problems that the church wrestles with as it lives in a world still broken but already redeemed by God will reflect the tension inherent in the two Trinitarian principles.

The church, being larger than a family or a marriage, is also far more complex. We can expect that the tensions in working out a harmony between these two principles will be far more complex in the church as well. The challenges will occur on all levels of the church's life. They occur on the level of the individual member as each member seeks to express his and her own distinct individuality as part of the larger congregation. The local church strives to develop a sense of unity in spirit and purpose among its members while valuing the wide diversity of its individual personalities. A congregation develops a personality of its own that comes to expression, while still being a part of the broader denomination to which it belongs. Each denomination has its own history, its struggles, interests, concerns, and limitations that make it distinct from the others, yet each denomination sees itself as belonging to the Body of Christ as a whole. And the church as a whole exists in the world, and yet separate from the world, with its own distinct identity. The church seeks to maintain a sense of its own distinctness from the world while still claiming to belong in this world which itself belongs to the God who redeemed it.

On each of these levels the potential for conflict and tension is present. Through all of this we are dealing with the holiness of the church, with the brokenness of the church, and with the wholeness that belongs to the responsiveness of the church.

The Holiness of the Church

How is the church to understand its own holiness? When we confess of the universal church that we believe in the "*holy* catholic church," what are we saying about the church—and, therefore, about ourselves who belong to the church? And how does what we say about ourselves in this regard affect our capacity to become increasingly responsive to God and to others both within and outside the church?

We are tempted to relate holiness to some degree of moral superiority that the church possesses, or to a higher spiritual attainment that belongs to the church, or to the purity of our confession of the truth. In thinking of the holiness of the church we are prone to contrast the church as holy with others who are unholy. We then create distance between us and those outside the church, and we relate to them condescendingly. We will treat other persons as objects whom we must change. They must become like us if they are to be worthwhile or "saved." Our own holiness then becomes the measure of what is good for others.

But tasting and sharing good "apples" may create further brokenness. Holiness begins to look suspiciously like the original sin—making ourselves the measure of what is good and right. As we yield to this temptation, we embrace our own righteousness—a righteousness like that of the Pharisees rather than the righteousness of the kingdom of God. Our "holiness" then inherently restricts our capacity to be responsive to others and to God. It restricts our faith, our hope, and our love, instead of enhancing them.

To confess the holiness of the church is to say something

significant about how God is at work in a world already redeemed by Christ. By his Holy Spirit God calls the church out of the world to himself. He restores faith to his people. He gives them a distinct identity as his own people. It is that identity, that relation to God, which comprises the holiness of the church.

Holiness, therefore, has to do with the church's confession of God's grace, with Christ's–and not our–righteousness. The distinctness of the church is that she has been called "chosen," embraced by God in Christ through the Holy Spirit. The church needs to cultivate a deep sense of being called out of the world, of being separated from the world, and of being set apart by God for his own purpose. The holiness of the church thus also has everything to do with the mission and purpose of the church in relation to the world.

Many of the names and metaphors applied to the church highlight the distinctness of the church in its separation from, and relation to, the world. Consider I Peter 2:9. "But you are [1] a chosen race, [2]a royal priesthood, [3]a holy nation, [4]God's own people, that you may declare the wonderful deeds of him who called you out of darkness into his marvelous light." The people of God are [5]"the salt of the earth" and [6]"the light of the world" (Matt.5:13-14). The church is [7]"the household of God" (Eph. 2:19) and [8]"the pillar and ground of the truth" (I Tim. 3:15).

All of these images can be summed up by saying that the church has been separated out from the world to be a community of faith, a people who once again trust in God and his sovereign grace. The church is the light of the world because it knows the Light. She is the pillar of the truth because she belongs to him who is the Truth. This separation from the world implies a separation from the darkness and perversion and deceit that characterizes the disjointed world.

What characterizes the world, on the other hand, can be described as its disengagement and enmeshment. Each of these opposite tendencies breaks trust and destroys community, blocking responsive growth.

Disengagement occurs when each individual is concerned only with his or her own good. Each lives as if he or she is the only measure of what is right and good. Everyone does what is right in his own eyes (cf. Judges 21:25). That applies to individuals, but it applies to larger social, racial, and national groupings as well. These larger groups, too, can each make their own group the measure of what is right and wrong, as races and nations commonly do over against others. In this broader disengagement lies the source of social unrest, of racial bigotry, and of wars among nations and between ethnic groups.

Enmeshment appears to be the opposite. It builds a community or a state in which everyone is coerced into thinking, feeling, doing, valuing the same things. No one is encouraged or allowed to develop in distinctly individual ways. Expressing a dissenting viewpoint may lead one to prison, if not to execution. Closed and tyrannical societies are aptly characterized in this way.

The ways of the world–disengagement and enmeshment–limit and undermine the responsivity for which we were created. They destroy faith and trust. They prevent the building of a community of trust. They are opposed to the purpose of the kingdom of God.

God calls the church to come out of the disengagement and the enmeshment, the brokenness, that characterizes the world. He calls the church to be his own people who believe, who trust, who have faith. He calls us to build a community of faith which will again grow in responsivity. The trust that was broken and lost by the fall into sin is restored in the church. The unique task of the church is to embody, as the Body of Christ, that renewal of trust. The church confesses its faith, its trust in God, by confessing that Jesus, the Christ of God, brings a kingdom which is not *of* this world, but which comes *to* this world and belongs *in* the world. What distinguishes the holiness of his body, the church, is that it proclaims and participates in his kingdom and its righteousness through the renewed responsiveness of faith.

But the church expresses her trust in God in strange ways. She does so not by claiming moral and spiritual superiority over others, but first of all through confession of sin. She does so secondly by turning again to the world from which she was separated, turning to embrace that world as already redeemed by God. Acknowledging her own brokenness prevents the church from glibly judging and condemning the world for its brokenness. Experiencing her own need for grace enables the church to see a world also desperately needing light, needing "salt," needing the clarity of truth. Trust is the mortar which holds together the bricks of the new "building," which then reaches out to embrace the world—the world with which the church seeks a new wholeness which will be enriching to both alike.

The holiness of the church follows a pathway leading through the confession of sin, outward toward a new wholeness which belongs to the kingdom of heaven. This mission gives the church her distinctive character and calling in the world.

The Brokenness of the Church

Rather than contradicting holiness, the confession of its own brokenness is one of the distinctive marks that belong to the church's holiness.

The Heidelberg Catechism, coming out of the sixteenth-century Reformation, makes some remarkable statements about the faith and life of the Christian Church. After explaining the meaning of the articles of faith found in the Apostles' Creed concerning the Father, the Son, and the Holy Spirit, it goes on to ask what the benefit is in believing all of this. The answer is that Christ's righteousness becomes ours "by faith alone" (Lord's Day 23, Q & A #61). It emphasizes that it is "not because of any value my faith has that God is pleased with me." In the next answer the Catechism elaborates by confessing that "even the very best we do in this life is imperfect and stained with sin" (Q & A #62). Because of that impurity of even our best works, our faith claims for itself no value for inducing God to be pleased with us more than with others.

When this confession of sin is taken seriously, what are the implications for understanding the distinct identity of the church in the world? That distinctiveness cannot be found in the quality of the church's faith and the purity of its doctrinal positions, in the sincerity of its worship, sacramental observance, and liturgies, or in the high quality of its preaching or excellent pastoral care. Nor can it be found in the church's lofty moral life and works, or in the moral integrity and spiritual sensitivity of her members. Where any of these are present in her there is reason for gratitude, but not for boasting. The church's faith and life at its best has no value for persuading God to favor her. All her best practices or works are acknowledged to be stained with sin. With that as our confession, we can place Christian faith and life alongside any other religious faith in the world, or alongside humanism, agnosticism, or even atheism, and we will find no value in our faith that makes us more pleasing to God than any of these others are.

It is not enough that we confess that the church has at times made grievous mistakes. We can readily cite examples of the church at its worst to illustrate sinfulness in the church. We can talk about the bloody crusades, the growing corruption of the church in the Middle Ages, the Inquisition, burnings at the stake, the Holocaust, and the Elmer Gantry's of contemporary television evangelism. We can also cite numerous examples of hypocrisy among ordinary members in the church. We can discover questionable or mixed motivations even in ourselves. But we are also invited to identify sin's stain in all of the church's most noble works, including its confession of faith at its very best. Two questions then arise. First, where in the best of the church's works, or those of its members, is this stain to be found so that it may be confessed? And second, when this pollution is recognized and confessed, how does that confession affect the church's responsiveness within the church and toward the world?

Sin is found in the breaking of trust. And that occurs wherever we make something good in ourselves the absolute measure of what is right and good and true for others. Sin is found in good "apples," nourishing "apples," that we reach out for and make our own. Indeed, sin may be found in the very best of our works when we turn our possession of them into a measure by which we judge and condemn those who do not possess them as we do. Then our good works, our faith itself, becomes a source of contention and strife, of division and brokenness. Not only has that occurred repeatedly throughout the history of the church—it continues to occur to this day. The best that is ours in this way becomes defiled with sin.

The Reformation, for example, rediscovered the biblical meaning and truth of "justification by faith." But before the sixteenth century was over, Calvinists and Lutherans began fighting not just with Rome but with each other over who possessed the "right" understanding of justification, of the real presence of Christ in the sacraments, and of the so-called "communication of attributes" in the human nature of Christ. And they could not live in the same church together with those whom they judged to be "wrong." These same reformers argued heatedly with the Anabaptists over who best understood the relationship of the church to the state, and who was right about baptizing or not baptizing infants. The crucial questions always came down to questions of who was right and who was wrong. Being "right like us" became the grounds for fellowship and unity in faith on all sides. It became the grounds for dismembering the Body of Christ. This reenactment of the original sin has occurred over almost all of the doctrines of the church and over many of the practices in the life of the church. Invariably we turn the truth of the gospel into a righteousness of our own that divides and adds to the brokenness of life. Protestant churches have thus ended up doing, themselves, the very thing they accused the Roman church of doing—following a human righteousness rather than the righteousness of God.

When sin in this way permeates the faith and life of the church, our capacity to be responsive to each other out of faith and love is severely diminished, if not lost. To be sure, after four centuries those old issues stir few souls and little passion today, but, despite Paul's warnings about the mind and the works of the flesh versus the fruit of the spirit (Gal. 5), fresh controversies continue to rage today and to tear churches apart with new divisions and further brokenness. Many of the contemporary issues cut across all denominational lines.

Let's reflect on some of the major controversies of our time: the dispute over Scripture, the creation/evolution debate, women in church office, abortion, and homosexuality. Our concern here is not with anything near an exhaustive treatment of these issues. The question in each instance is simply this: Where does the error, the stain of sinfulness, lie in our dealing with these issues? How is it that we deal with these issues in a way that leads us to become less rather than more responsive to each other as we come to differing conclusions on the issues? And is it possible to take all of these issues seriously and still become increasingly responsive to each other? Might we even gratefully enhance each other's growth through our differences?

The Battle over the Bible

Nowhere has the brokenness of the church become more evident than in strife over the Scriptures. For several years the

Southern Baptist Church has experienced a power struggle between conservatives and moderates for control over the various institutions of that denomination. Some years ago the Missouri Synod of the Lutheran Church split when seminary professors were fired because they did not have the "right" view of Scripture. Other denominations have experienced their own tensions over this issue. The irony here is that the more one espouses what is called a "high" (that is, "right") view of Scripture, the more narrow appears to be one's capacity to respond in love toward fellow Christians with differing views.

The problem does not lie in the fact that disagreements occur over what is the best way to characterize the Bible as the Word of God. Such disagreements can produce growing insight for all. Each side can provide a healthy balance to the possible excesses on the other side. Nor is the real problem the fact that someone has to be in error somewhere, since both sides cannot be right. Being wrong may produce distorted insight and may diminish one's ability to respond to others appropriately or in love, but being wrong has never been a barrier to entering the kingdom of God—else no one would ever enter.

The error or "stain" in a view of Scripture may not lie primarily in its being wrong. No, it is making one's own "right" view the measure for acceptance and fellowship that reproduces the original sin. What is more, as we insist that our "right" view is the only legitimate one, two other consequences will follow.

First, our energy will increasingly be poured into "proving" (that is, marshalling arguments to support our view) that our doctrine of Scripture is right and someone else's is wrong. Our attention will focus on what we and others say about Scripture rather than listening to what the Scriptures are saying to us. The Bible's message to us is that our being right does not bring us even to the entryway of the kingdom of God. Only God's way of doing right—embracing wrong-headed sinners like us—brings in the kingdom. Ignoring the message, we pass the whole of Scripture through a filter of our own making which will yield instructions only on what we must do right in all areas of life—morally, spiritually, theologically, and ecclesiastically. We turn the Scriptures into a how-to-do-it manual for producing more of our own righteousness. In this way we miss the gateway to the kingdom of heaven (cf. Matt. 5:20).

Second, our own responsivity becomes increasingly rigidified. Focusing on what we must do right, we find it hard to hear and respond to the gospel as the good news from God that it is. We do not acknowledge that our own responsiveness comes into play as we read the Scriptures. We do not allow room for the responsiveness of others to express itself freely and creatively. And we diminish our capacity to respond with understanding, concern, acceptance, and love toward fellow Christians who differ from us.

This process occurs on all sides of the issue. It is not just those who insist on a narrow view of inerrancy and literalism whose responsiveness becomes limited. Those who endorse a more moderate or a liberal view of the Scriptures can be just as unresponsive toward fundamentalists and others who differ from them. What we are then left with is a sense of sin's stain which invades the church's simple confession of faith in the word of Scripture.

But what happens to a church which comes to recognize and confess the stain of sin in the best of its works—even in our profession of faith in the Scriptures as the Word of God? We stop fighting. We continue to share and disagree on our insights into the Scriptures, but we clearly see our insights as part of our own responsiveness to the Scriptures and therefore never as the final word. We become more open to each other and less judgmental. We begin to benefit and learn from each other in those areas of disagreement, even when we are convinced that another is missing the heart of the gospel. Thus we more truly bear witness to a gospel that is good news—first of all for us, but also for the whole world because it is based not on our getting it right, but on the righteousness that is revealed from God. That is where the power of the gospel lies! (cf. Rom. 1:16-17)

The Creation/Evolution Debate

One of the most fascinating debates in recent history continues to be that over the origin of the universe, and of human beings in particular. What is troubling here is what happens to the nature of faith when we insist that any notion of an evolutionary development of human beings from animals necessarily involves a denial of faith.

The central meaning of faith involves trust. We live by faith when we live in trust, first of all toward God, but then also toward one another. The problem is not with those creationists who express their faith by saying that, for them, trust in God is inextricably bound up with a God who creates human beings out of dust and not out of previously existing animals. Such a viewpoint may well be a legitimate response to the Biblical word in the context of long-held beliefs. It may be a genuine expression of faith, an act of trust in the Creator-God. We can all affirm that faith, even if we disagree in our scientific perspectives.

In the anti-evolutionary debate, however, the matter of trust is often no longer the relevant issue. The focus of the debate is simply on the question of who is right. And when our being right becomes the crucial issue, trust further breaks down among fellow Christians. Even if creationists should in the end prove to be right, they are wrong in making their own right the measure of "faith" for all–and the basis of fellowship together.

When we make our own right ideas–on either side of the issue– the measure of truth, we diminish our capacity to be responsive to others in trust and love. But something more occurs. We also limit our capacity to interact with and reflect imaginatively on the whole created world over which God has entrusted dominion to us.

The confession of the church is that the best of our scientific and theological works are stained with sin. That includes all of our reflecting on the processes of creation. Such a confession can help us regain our responsivity both to the creation itself and to those with whom we disagree. Taking our own "right" views with less absolute seriousness can lead to a growing openness both to the creation itself and to each other in our differing understandings and conclusions.

Women in Church Office

It belongs to the church's confession to acknowledge that sin's brokenness also reaches into the relationship of men and women within the church. Breaking trust with the sovereign Creator by making ourselves the measure of what is right, we cannot sustain trust between the sexes. Our responsivity toward each other as male and female has diminished. Instead of enhancing each other's growth and delighting in that development wherever we discover it, we manipulate and limit each other as men and women in countless ways. In the process we limit ourselves, too, since in excluding women from church office men thereby deprive the church of women's feminine perspective. And it is not only men and women who relate to each other with diminished responsiveness; men also take sides against other men, and women against other women, as the issue heats up.

The issue of barring women from office in the church brings to the fore several ways in which our responsivity has been blocked.

A Restrictive Hermeneutic: A hermeneutic which concludes that women should be barred from holding church office is one which narrowly looks at various isolated verses of Scripture, to distill from them the rules that we must keep if we are to do things right, whether in our individual lives or as a church. We focus on two or three key texts about women keeping silent in the church, and then argue whether or not these texts forbid women to hold office. Other biblical material from creation and the fall, from the history of Israel and the life of Jesus, as well as from other concerns expressed by Paul, are then interpreted according to the rule distilled from the key proof texts. Any real listening to the central and full message of the gospel throughout the Scriptures is blocked out or at best considered irrelevant to the issue of office-bearing. Our concern with determining the "right rules" obstructs responsiveness and openness to the message of the Scriptures as we oppose those who differ from us and thus are considered to be wrong.

A Denial of Our Responsivity: Having restricted our way of reading Scripture, we also tend to deny the role that our own responsiveness plays in interpreting what the Scriptures say about women. We accuse others of being influenced by the cultural trends of our time such as secular feminism, but we blind ourselves to the ways in which we ourselves are influenced by our tradition and our upbringing, by sexual stereotypes and other biases against what is unfamiliar, and by the intellectual and cultural climate of our times. This denial of our own responsivity in interpreting the Scriptures is in reality a flight from accountability. We hide behind the smokescreen of objectivity, needing the illusion of objectivity to make our own interpretations the measure of truth, so that we can then directly equate our own responses regarding the place of women in the church with God's word and will. We thus invent another way to make ourselves like God in knowing good and evil.

A Denial of Responsivity in Our Heritage: Some who adamantly oppose women holding office in the church point to the long history of the church in which women have been excluded from office. Are we to suppose, they ask, that the church has been wrong all these years and that we alone have suddenly discovered the truth? This frequently heard question reveals the supposition that the issue is simply a matter of who is right and who is wrong. In reality our forebears in the church were responding to the Scriptures out of who they were in the context in which they lived, with the current wisdom and understanding that was theirs. In this regard they were no different then than we are now. They, however, had the humility to acknowledge that the best of their works were stained with sin—something in them, as in ourselves, to which we may be blinded when we idealize them.

A Restricted Responsivity toward Opponents: When the primary concern in the women's issue becomes that of proving that we are right and others wrong, we lose much of our capacity to respond with caring toward those who take a view other than our own. We lose our willingness, if not our ability, to listen to the concerns that others have that we may have overlooked. When we are not listening to and willing to learn from them, we increase the likelihood that they will also not hear our concerns or be willing to learn from us. Each side then attributes motives and influences to the other which have little bearing on what the other is actually saying. We become polarized. We then get to the point of having to judge and condemn and withdraw from each other in order to justify our own position. As we move toward this point, we are once again ready to dismember the Body of Christ.

A Restricted Responsivity toward Women: Part of the problem with the debate over whether or not women should hold office in the church is that the debate itself may diminish responsiveness within the church toward women. The more focused we are on proving that we are right and others wrong, the less sensitive we are likely to become to the hurt and pain that women have been experiencing in the church, as well as in society. How women feel, we are told, is not the issue, but only what the Scriptures teach. In the name of our "getting it right" we justify being unresponsive to the injustice that women experience. We can, moreover, invest so much energy in debating the theology of women that we have no energy left for improving the opportunities for women to share fully in the life of the church. I recall a point, several years ago when I was devoting a considerable amount of time to writing on the women's issue, that my wife found it necessary to chide me, saying, "You can write all you want in favor of women, but you seem to have no time left for me or the children!" It was a valuable lesson in coming to understand something of what is meant by confessing that the best of our works are stained with sin.

The women's issue in the church is thus one which amply demonstrates the brokenness of the church. The breakdown in our capacity to be responsive to each other as men and women in the church prevents us from valuing and celebrating the differences between us in such a way that our relationships enhance the identity and position of each. It may be debatable whether the record of the church is worse or better than that of society at large. Yet the holiness of the church, her distinctness from the world, lies not in her getting it right, but in her being called to confession of sin as the way toward a new wholeness.

The Abortion Debate

No issue confronting the church and society stirs deeper passions in its advocates than does the Pro-Life position on the one hand and the Pro-Choice position on the other. But for that very reason this issue clearly demonstrates the brokenness of the church as well as that of society at large. The more each side is convinced of the rightness of its own viewpoint, the more justified each seems to feel in assaulting the other side. Each side appears incapable of being in any way responsive to the concerns of the other side. And that is the case not just in the secular world, but especially, it would seem, in the church itself.

We are dealing here with more than a debate over theory. One paradox is that the more convinced any individual or group is that their position on abortion is right, the less capable they seem to be of responding with sensitivity toward human life on the other side. Those who uphold the principle of choice, along with those who glibly seek out an abortion, appear at times to be callous to the life that is growing in the womb. And those who claim to be pro-life sometimes show enormous insensitivity to women who are painfully struggling with a difficult choice.

It is one thing to have strong convictions about what is morally right and what is morally wrong in the matter of abortion. But drawing conclusions about what is right may be the easiest part of the moral process. The really profound moral challenge is not that of deciding what is right. The deepest moral choice that all of us confront is that of determining how we, personally, can relate most responsively to a woman who is considering or has had an abortion. We have many choices. Screaming "Murderer!" at her is one choice. We can hassle and taunt her as she enters a clinic. We can ridicule and condemn her. We can shun her in her struggle and ostracize her afterward. We can try to talk her out of an abortion, using a variety of tones. We can try to persuade her to carry the pregnancy to full term and give the baby up for adoption. We can offer help with the baby if she chooses to keep it. We can listen with empathy to her pain. We can explore various options with her and help her sort them out for herself. We can encourage her and support her in her choice of abortion. We can attempt to talk her into an abortion even if she is reluctant. It is not only the woman with an unwanted pregnancy who faces moral choices. Every one of us faces our own moral choices as we interact with her. We have a wide range of ways in which we can choose how to be responsive. What we cannot do is choose not to be responsive. The moral question we face is whether the responses we give will promote or hinder her growth in responsiveness and ours.

The church could deal more compassionately with women who seek abortion if we would recognize the two positions as each representing one of two basic Christian principles: One—God is our sovereign Creator; life therefore is holy and demands respect because he created it. Two—God created us to be responsive. The exercise of our choices belongs to our responsivity; take away human choice, and you destroy human responsivity and diminish human life. The Pro-Life and Pro-Choice positions are in deep tension with each other in much the same way that the recognition of divine sovereignty and the affirmation of human responsibility have always been in tension. With great difficulty the church has tried always to honor both principles together.

We need not pit one side angrily against the other in the Pro-Life vs. Pro-Choice debate. We can instead affirm values on both sides, even as we recognize that the church itself is splintered today over this issue. Our responsiveness falls short on all sides. The distinctive calling of the church is to stand before God and the world confessing the sin of insensitivity. Within that stance of confession we may find it a little harder to respond with condemnation of those we judge to be sinners or to be wrong. Confessing our own sin opens the way to new forms of responsiveness, responses of compassion and understanding, toward those with whom we may disagree. With new eyes we can now see them to be struggling, hurting human beings much like ourselves.

Homosexuality

The discussion of human sexuality, and homosexuality in particular, is likely to contribute its share to the brokenness of the church well into the present century. Several major denominations continue to struggle with the question of the legitimacy of homosexuality. Many of us have difficulty knowing how to be responsive to homosexual persons and to the gay movement. We also have trouble responding positively toward those who take a different stance on this issue than we do. We largely limit our responses to avoiding, condemning, and trying to control or change those whose opinions differ from ours.

Here we again have two distinguishable questions to deal with. One is the theoretical, ethical position which we can formulate in study reports where we try to determine whether a distinction between sexual orientation and sexual practice is a valid and helpful one, and whether some form of committed homosexual relationship is justified. The other question has to do with our relationships: How do I, and how does the church, relate to specific individuals who are known or thought to be practicing homosexuals? Can we accept them into our social circle and into our congregational life? Can we welcome them into the offices of the church?

In answer to the theoretical question, if we justify homosexual relations ethically we may seek to develop friendships with homosexual persons and invite them into our church circles. On the other hand, if we have decided that homosexual activity is morally wrong, we may do everything we can to keep gays out of the church and as far away from us as possible.

In answer to the question of relating on a personal basis, we may already have established a friendship with a homosexual individual and on that basis proceed to justify the practice morally as if nothing more than an alternative life-style is involved. Or, starting with a gut-level revulsion toward even the thought of gay activity, we may automatically consider homosexual activity to be morally wrong without further reflection.

One way to approach these questions is to start with a conviction that confession of sin is the pathway to holiness and wholeness. Paul takes this approach in his letter to the Romans. He asserts that the gospel's power lies not in our own right ways but in God's righteousness (1:16-17). God's wrath is revealed against all the ways in which we get it wrong (1:18). Paul begins with our idolatry, in which we worship good things that are not good enough ("worshipped and served the creature rather than the Creator" vs. 25) because they are not God (1:19-23). As God gives us over to our own ways, says Paul, we fall into sexual distortions in both heterosexual and homosexual practices as we seek to experience and to share the enjoyment of our sexuality (1:26-27). But as God continues to turn us over to our own ways, we begin to know the full depths of sin's degradation. Here we no longer seek after what is inherently good, though sadly distorted; giving up the pursuit of what is good, we develop a really "base mind" as we seek to hurt one another. We become full of envy, strife, deceit, and murder; we gossip and slander; we become foolish and faithless, heartless and ruthless (1:28-32). The practice of gossip, Paul seems to say, more deeply reveals the base mind than does homosexual activity.

Why would Paul be telling us all this? His purpose is to lead us beyond judging others–idolaters, homosexuals, murderers. In condemning the homosexual, he says, we are condemning ourselves. He brings us to the point of confessing our own sin and of relying not on our getting sexual issues right, but on Christ's righteousness and on God's grace alone (2:1 ff; 3:21 ff). Confession provides the church with new perspectives for dealing with the issue of homosexuality.

None of us escapes the unnatural state of human life in this world of broken responsivity. Who of us is able to judge another without ourselves thereby being judged (Rom. 2:1)? Being embraced by Jesus' righteousness enables us to face and confess our own sin and brokenness. Only as we do so can we also see the brokenness in others without having to condemn and push away. God's love kindles a new responsiveness within us. However imperfectly we may do it, we can still value others in their brokenness. We can value, as well, those whose limited and broken responsiveness does not yet allow them to accept and live with homosexual persons in the church and in society. We can even value ourselves with our own limited and broken responsiveness.

Wholeness in the Church

The more responsive the church is to God, the more that responsiveness grows among the distinct and diverse members within her ranks. But responsiveness then also moves outward from the church toward the world which, even in its brokenness, still belongs to God. The new responsiveness that comes from faith in God's grace and his righteousness, and from confession of our sin, produces a twofold wholeness: a growing wholeness within the church, and a new and growing wholeness with the world from which the church was separated out.

Within the Church

Wholeness is a vision that is already present and at work within the church on all levels and in all dimensions of her existence. The church attains only a small beginning in the realization of that wholeness. Yet, as we turn repeatedly to confession of our broken righteousness, and as we renew trust in the righteousness by which God embraces those who are broken, healing occurs and wholeness grows.

<u>Preaching</u>: Preaching is not just the subjective opinions of the preacher offered to the congregation to do with as the members please. Neither is preaching simply the objective word from God which the preacher can deliver to the people as if his words and God's are one and the same and the people must obey

him unquestioningly. If preaching is only the former, it will lack authenticity and have little that is compelling in it. If it is only the latter, it will become a form of idolatrous manipulation.

A sermon is always the proclamation of the good news. As such, the sermon becomes the channel for conveying the message of God's righteousness and grace which evokes in the listener a new or renewed responsiveness both toward God and toward others. The more sermonizing either tends to become subjective or pretends to be purely objective, the more such sermons will focus on what we can and must do right rather than on how God in Christ has already set things right. Sermons will then degenerate into subjective moralizing or objective intellectualizing rather than being the proclamation of grace.

To avoid both subjectivism and objectivism, we need to recognize that the preacher is both listening to the word of God and giving his own response to it. If he is not listening to what God is saying, his sermon will be a message from him- (or her) self rather than from God. But if he claims to be bringing a purely objective message from God, his own responsiveness to both the Word of God and to the people of his congregation will be limited and rigid.

The congregation hearing the preaching of the Word needs a keen sense that the Word of God's grace is neither the subjective ideas of the preacher nor objective truths that only need to be agreed with. The message of the Word of God's righteousness and grace calls forth a response from those who hear it. Because it is a Word that evokes confession of sin in ourselves and proclaims God's gracious embrace of sinners, such preaching will inspire its hearers to respond to one another in forgiving love and acceptance. Where preaching is the proclamation of God's rather than our righteousness, it brings healing and wholeness to the lives of individuals as well as to the congregation. The congregation then becomes a healing community where trust grows.

Because human responsivity is always present and is called forth and enhanced by the sovereign Word of grace, we can expect and delight in the differences among preachers whose sermons proclaim the same Word in differing ways, and among the hearers who hear the Word each in his or her own way. Such differences do not undermine the unity of the church, but contribute to and enrich its wholeness.

Worship and Liturgy: Worship is our human response to God's grace. It is more than just listening to preaching, more than trying to find a prescription for what we must do right to be acceptable. The more fully God's goodness is seen both in creation and in redemption, the more the responsiveness of the congregation will come to joyful expression in our worship, even in the liturgical confession of sin.

The entire liturgy involves the congregation's personal and communal response to the sovereign God of grace. The manner in which individuals within the same congregation, and congregations from different cultural or denominational backgrounds, express their liturgical response to God will be diverse; that diversity will be enhancing to all of us as we experience more of it. The differing forms of liturgical worship can be viewed not as threatening the unity of the church, but as enriching it.

Congregational Life: What we observed about preaching and about worship applies to all aspects of congregational life. The educational program for children and adults, the gatherings that promote fellowship, the service projects, the evangelism and world missions efforts, and the ecumenical endeavors of the congregation all represent the church's response to the gracious working of God. These responses will always be incomplete and leave room for correction and growth as well as for widely differing developments among differing congregations within a denomination and among denominations. Rather than being a reason for dissension and division, these differences can be appreciated as a source of enrichment to the whole church of God throughout the world, regardless of how they originated.

Whatever occurs within a congregation belongs to the church's response to God's grace. That includes the ongoing confession of how our own responsivity to God and to each other is blocked by the many ways in which we subtly or blatantly focus on our own righteousness as decisive, and therefore divisive. When our faith is focused on God's righteousness and grace, then our concern can freely be directed to what enhances responsiveness in each person and in the church as a whole, ministering also to those who are suffering from physical, mental, or emotional problems. To enable and enhance this growth, God has called his church to come apart from the world–to be separate and holy.

The distinctness of the church, however, is never an end in itself. As the church gains a sense of her own identity, she sees her mission to be that of turning again to the world from which she was called out. She can now preach the gospel as good news to the whole world, calling people everywhere to turn in faith to trust the sovereign God of grace, mercy, and peace. The church does not reject and condemn the broken world that God loves, but seeks reconciliation and wholeness for and with the world.

Between Church and World

Some of the names or images applied to the church in the New Testament indicate the separateness of the church in her distinctness from the world: she is "a chosen race" and "a holy nation." Other images suggest the close relationship of the church to God: she is "the household of God," that is, "God's own people" (cf. I Peter 2:9 and I Tim. 3:15).

Still other images, however, express the relationship of the church to the world as the church turns back toward the world. The church is "the light of the world" and "the salt of the earth" (cf. Matt. 5:13-14). She is also "a royal priesthood" (I Peter 2:9) and "the pillar and bulwark of the truth" (I Tim. 3:15). In these metaphors we see again that the separations that God effects are very different from the separations that we bring about. *We* cause separations in the church that produce no healing and create no renewed wholeness. When *God* separates out the church from the world there is healing and hope. Just as in creation he originally separated the light from the darkness, God recreates a new wholeness between the church and the world.

Light never exists only for its own sake. Even in the creation of the sun and moon, God set these lights in the sky in order to give light upon the earth. In their separateness, sun and moon are beautiful creations, enhancing the earth as they illumine it, but God is at least as interested in the earth as he is in the sun and moon. When Chicago's Wrigley Field finally received lights that could be turned on at night, people came out not just to admire the new lights, but rather to see the Cubs play baseball at night under the illumination of the lights. The ballgame was what was important. We can view the role of the church in the same way. She is called out of the world to be God's own people, a light in the midst of a dark world. The light shines on the world because it is a world that belongs to God. God is not interested in the church as a light just for its own sake. He wants this whole world to be illumined with light because it is the world that he values and loves. After all, he created this world, and loved it so much that he gave his only begotten son to redeem it.

And as to being the "salt of the earth," how would you like to have a meal that began with appetizers of just salt? And then be served a main course of a heaping plate of salt? And then for dessert another portion of salt? That would not be my choice, nor is it God's. We may use salt as a preservative to keep meat from going bad, but it is the meat that we value and want to preserve. We use salt to enhance the flavor of much of the food that we eat, but it is the food with its variety of tastes and textures that we want to enjoy. So it is with the church and the world. We who are the chosen people of God are called out of the world and given our own identity as salt. We then return to the world that God loves and has redeemed, to enhance that world by preserving and seasoning it so that God may be well pleased with the whole world as a delight to his taste.

"A royal priesthood" stands between God and the world. God does not appoint priests for their own sake. He did not appoint all Israel to become Levitical priests. He appointed priests to stand between himself and the people, to bring the people to him. Nor does God now want all the world to become priests. The church's identity lies in being that royal priesthood. The church separates from the world by gathering together in order to intercede for the world that God loves. The church confesses before God the sins of the world. On behalf of the whole world the church gives voice to the praises that magnify the name of the sovereign Lord of heaven and earth. The existence of the church as a royal priesthood stands as a testimony to the worth of the world that belongs to God and has been redeemed by him.

The church is, therefore, the pillar and ground of the truth. And the truth of which she is the pillar is that the power of God to bring salvation or wholeness lies not in our doing something right, but in the righteousness of God who embraces a broken world as his own world. The truth that the world needs to hear in its brokenness is that God values the world and the peoples of the world. The church as a royal priesthood, as salt, and as light, embodies that truth as she goes into all the world to proclaim the good news of the kingdom and its righteousness and to participate in that righteousness. The church participates by reaching out and embracing the world and its broken peoples with the love of God. The church's mission is to be the strong arms of God, the tender arms of Christ, arms that embrace the world in the responsiveness of trust, hope, and love. Embraced by the arms of the Body of Christ, the world learns what it means to trust and to have hope and to love. We thus "become the righteousness of God" to the world (II Corinthians 5:21). As the church embodies the servant mind of Christ, she looks forward to the day when "at the name of Jesus every knee shall bow…and every tongue confess that Jesus Christ is Lord, to the glory of God the Father" (Philippians 2:10-11). Only when that day arrives will the circle of trust and love be fully restored and made whole again.

Summary

The Trinitarian model promotes the growth of responsivity on all levels of the church's life. It gives a vision of the church's holiness. It provides the guidelines for dealing with difficult issues like hermeneutics, evolution, women in office, abortion, and homosexuality. It was not only in the past that the Body of Christ was torn apart. What still destroys today is not any one issue in itself, nor all of them together. The presence of deeply felt disagreements is not what divides us. What tears the church apart, today as in the past, is the insistence that we alone are right and others wrong—with our right being the measure of whether fellowship in Christ is possible. Strife and divisions in the body of Christ always proceed from an insistence on our own righteousness, never from the healing righteousness of heaven's kingdom.

No amount of brokenness, however, detracts from the church's distinctness from the world. The church is called first of all to come out and be separate by confessing rather than justifying her own "disengagement" and "enmeshment"–her sin. Through the pathway of confession of sin, the responsiveness evoked by the gracious embrace of God in his mercy and love leads to individual healing and to a growing wholeness within the body of Christ. A heightened awareness of her own brokenness enables the church to be responsive in a growing measure to the God whose sovereign grace alone can be trusted as the fountain of salvation, of wholeness—to the church first, and also to a world already redeemed by Christ.

We then return to a still-broken world, but we see with new eyes, opened to God's kingdom and his righteousness. We discover a world that we can value even as we see more clearly the stark reality of its brokenness. We have a mission.

Living out that mission, we can now go on to explore something of what it means to live responsively in a broken world which has already been redeemed by Christ.

10

LIVING RESPONSIVELY
in **THE WORLD**

What we call "the world" is an extremely complex phenomenon. The sovereign Lord of heaven and earth has created us in his own image so that we will be responsive to him, yes, and to each other in marital and family and church relationships. But more than that, he has created us to be responsive to the whole of his creation, the world in which we live. Let's take a brief tour of that vast and complicated world.

A small planet revolving around a middle-sized star is our home. Together we travel among millions of other stars around our Milky Way, a galaxy of stars which itself belongs to a cluster of galaxies. Within our cosmos are thousands, perhaps millions, of such clusters of galaxies. Our current knowledge is only a tiny fragment of what there is to know about this expansive world in which we live.

Just as individual lives and family life both go through stages, so stars and galaxies appear to go through their own life cycles from birth to death. From big bang to black holes, from variable stars to quasars, our world elicits a response of wonder and curiosity and even fear as we attempt to formulate hypotheses about its workings. Closer to home, we are learning more about our immediate solar neighborhood as human beings land on the moon, as satellites circle the earth and fly by the various planets and their moons, and as the Hubble telescope, with its originally flawed but later corrected lens, reveals further secrets and amazing images of our universe.

Our fascination with Mother Earth grows deeper as we view her from outer space through photographs—this beautiful blue planet with swirls of white clouds that is our home. We worry about reported holes in the ozone layer and a predicted warming from the greenhouse effect. Here on the surface we experience the majesty of earth's mountains and the rich farmlands of her plains, we marvel at the breadth and depth of her seas teeming with life, and we are often refreshed by inland lakes and streams. Her forests are mysteriously dense, and her wildlife intriguing in all its variations. Many species are dangerous; others are endangered. Earth's resources seem almost infinite, but we wonder when they will be exhausted. We fear the power of hurricanes and tornadoes, the severity of floods and drought, the devastation of earthquakes and volcanoes. We are confronted by the pollution of earth's air and waterways and the diminishing of her rain forests. The earth is a home that is both hospitable to us and hostile, both fruitful and fragile. She is our world to live in, "to till and to keep." How shall we live responsively on this earth that is our home?

Our world is also the world of people, people who form many races and nations, each with their own rich heritage, traditions, religions, and cultures. All of them contribute something worthwhile to our own lives as we experience them. These nations also develop deep rivalries, long-standing animosities, and renewed distrust that lead to fresh outbreaks of hostility and warfare. This, too, belongs to the world in which we live.

We live in a world of scientific growth, expanding technology, and medical miracles. It's a world, also, of insightful literature and provocative art, of business and industrial development, of new educational and vocational opportunities in fields such as communications and computers and in a burgeoning service industry. Microchips and microprocessors, microphysics and microbiology, microorganisms and genetic engineering stir a sense of wonder at the world of small things. Ours is a world of big cities with magnificent skylines, of sprawling suburbs with luxurious living, and of large, mechanized farms cultivated with air-conditioned tractors. Joining all this together are ribbons of interstate highways, and buses, trains, and airplanes that speed us along our way. We live in a world of wealth.

We live, also, in a world of poverty, a world of the hungry

and the homeless, a world of cancer and heart disease and AIDS, a world of divorce and depression, a world of drugs and drunkenness and death on the highways. We live in a world of pornography and prostitution and promiscuity. The world we live in is a world of burglaries and assault and murder, a world of sexual harassment and rape. It is a world of racial discrimination, of political corruption, and of police brutality. It is a world of prisons and hospitals and cemeteries.

But first and foremost our world is the world of our own neighborhood, of our place of employment, of the friends and relatives who most significantly affect our lives. Sometimes it is for us a world of unemployment, of loneliness, of sickness, and of dying.

In short, our world includes so much that is good and beautiful and rewarding. And our world includes so much that is painful and threatening and disillusioning. How shall we live in such a world by faith? Created to be responsive, how shall we respond to all that makes up "the world?"

Responses to the World

There are as many ways of responding to the world as there have been persons living in the world. But it is helpful to identify in broad terms some typical ways in which Christians have tended to respond. Doing so helps us recognize those responses that limit our growth in responsivity and those that enhance our responsivity as we live in God's world. There are two ways of responding which begin with an affirmation of the world, but limit our religious responsiveness: (1) compartmentalizing religion and the world, and (2) civilizing religion. Two other responses take their stance in an affirmation of religious meanings, but diminish our appreciation for the world: (1) we can condemn and withdraw from the world, or, (2) we can seek to Christianize the world. Let's look briefly at each of these four ways of responding to the world. Then we will explore whether religious faith itself can lead to a more balanced appreciation of the world through confrontive celebration.

Compartmentalizing Religion and World

One way of living in the world is to treat "the world" and all matters of religion as if they belong in two separate compartments that have little or no interaction or relationship. Religious faith will then have little or no bearing on how we perceive or interact with that world in its many dimensions. We are then free to respond to the world in any way we choose or feel compelled to do. From this position we can affirm religious faith, we can consider it unimportant, or we can reject it outright.

We may compartmentalize religion and the world by affirming the value of religious faith as a purely personal or private affair. Such a faith may give us a sense of comfort or hope, but it will have no bearing on how we view the sciences or participate in the arts or humanities, or how we regulate our lives in the broader areas of society.

But I may also decide that I have no personal need for religious faith. I can consider faith largely irrelevant for myself and yet respect anyone who personally values it. The two of us will get along quite fine together; we both agree that life in the world needs to be dealt with on its own terms without interference from religious faith. This is the viewpoint found in secularism.

Others will take an antagonistic attitude toward religious faith. They will oppose it actively. They will strike out against any attempt by religious people to express in the public domain the relevance of their faith. They will militate against any display of religiosity in public schools or in the symbols which towns and cities display in their city seals or allow on public property. They want a society which is devoid of any outward or public acknowledgment of God or of religious traditions. Some agnostics or atheists energetically pursue this course for social policy with unswerving zeal. Others, such as the humanists, are more sophisticated, merely refusing to allow any religious considerations to enter into their reflections of the world of science, the arts, or their understanding of the human spirit and human relationships.

In whatever form it occurs, we can recognize something worthwhile in this attempt to deal with the world. Throughout history religious "faith" has often exercised a form of tyranny over the arts and sciences and over the freedom of people to live fully in the world and experience it in all its fullness. Rejecting that tyranny, secularism and humanism have made significant contributions toward enhancing our capacity to respond to a world that God has created and redeemed.

At the same time, however, compartmentalizing "the world"

and "religion" places severe restrictions both on our capacity to seek out and experience religious meanings, and on the ways in which we may experience the world as a world which belongs to God.

Civilizing Religion

Still taking our stance primarily in an affirmation of the world and its values, we can seek to make religion and Christian faith relevant to the world by enlisting faith in the service of some particular aspect of the world that we consider to be of paramount importance.

We may, for example, turn religious faith into a powerful force for advancing a favored social or political philosophy. If we are politically and socially conservative, we may use religious faith to promote loyalty to these values; to be Christian, then, is almost equated with embracing a conservative economic policy and supporting the Republican Party in elections, and celebrating the superiority of the "American way of life." If we are more liberal in our politics and social policy, we may focus all the meaning of Christian faith on the issues of liberating the poor from the oppression of the rich; Christian faith is then relevant only to the extent that it furthers the endorsed objectives of this liberal socio-political movement.

We can make Christian faith "civilized" in other ways, too. The "health and wealth" brand of Christianity starts with the assumption that our achieving health and abundance is the primary good in life. Therefore God surely wants both of these for us; if we just have faith (and support the "evangelist" with our contributions) we are promised both.

In a more sophisticated way we can attempt to turn Christian faith into an affirmation of some psychological perspective. From an interest in psychology and mental health, for example, we may conclude that the most important issue in life is that of promoting self-esteem. We may then reinterpret all of Christian meanings and theology to be a message that encourages this important goal.

The value of these attempts to "civilize" religious faith lies in the desire to bring one's faith to bear on the world in some positive, relevant, and specific way. But the cost may be high. A civilized faith can easily lose its power to confront the evils and injustice of the world, and may lose much of its own distinctive character as Christian.

Condemning the World

As Christians we may be much impressed with the evil and the temptations to evil that are present in the world. From that stance our concern is not first of all with affirming the value of the world. We fear that affirmation of any aspect of the world will lead to a diminishing of our faith and spirituality. Our primary concern, then, is to affirm and cultivate the spiritual values which we derive from our faith in God and in Christ. We take our stand firmly in our religious faith, and we respond to the world by condemning it for its evils and by withdrawing from involvement in the world as much as possible. Here, too, we may do so in a variety of ways.

Some of us condemn the world not so much by railing against its evils, but by forming our own largely self-contained and self-sufficient religious communities so as to avoid "contamination" by the world as much as we can. We cannot avoid all contact with the products of civilization, but we can, in principle, make do with as little as possible from "the world." Thus we will make use of the wheel, the saw, and the hammer, but we will avoid the use of automobiles and chainsaws and most of the benefits of modern science and technology.

Others of us will not live apart from the world in separately formed communities but will live in the same cities and towns that the world forms; the primary thrust of our lives, however, will be to avoid "worldly" things. We may develop strong mores against "worldly" activities such as dancing and theater attendance and reading unwholesome books. Much of our energy will go into denouncing the evils of the world—materialism, pornography, gambling, illicit sex, or even humanistic science and philosophy. We consider the world to be under the power of Satan and his host of demons. We view as lost those who are not Christians like us; they are to be avoided except as we try to convert them. As Christians of this sort we are often devoutly sincere in our religious faith, and we may go to the ends of the earth to "save" others; there is thus a genuine element of caring and love in our responding to the people of the world. Yet our condemnation of the world limits our capacity to be responsive to much of the good that is present in the world as created and redeemed by God. Our religious faith seems to promote a self-limiting vision of the kingdom of God.

Christianizing the World

A fourth way of responding to the world also takes its starting point in the affirmation of Christian faith. Like the previous stance, this one also views the world as it exists apart from Christian faith to be a lost world, a world of sin and falsehood, of temptation and evil, a world that is opposed to the kingdom of God and exists in an antithetical relationship to God's rule. The City of God and the City of the World are forever at odds with each other. The one is redeemed, the other condemned.

This viewpoint is much more optimistic about the potential for good that is present in all of the world. The world in all of its complexity can be brought into subjection to Christ. All areas of the world's existence can be made to serve Christ and his kingdom. Christians must reclaim the world for Christ. We are called not to withdraw from the world but to enter into all areas of the world's life to "Christianize" them. As we bring these areas into Christ's service we build the kingdom of God.

In this way of responding to the world we do more than try to hold on to a compartmentalized faith as we live and do our work in the world. Living in the world as Christians, we do more than try to make converts out of non-Christians and believers out of unbelievers. Rather than being suspicious of too much education, for example, we seek to further the cause of education, though education in a public school is seen as permeated with secular humanism and therefore corrupting, so we set about establishing Christian schools. With the help of Christian textbooks, these schools are to give expression to a Christian view of life that can be taught to children in every area of study. We also establish institutions of higher learning—not only to train students to think as Christians, but to promote and contribute to the body of knowledge in all areas from a Christian perspective. Thus we respond to the world as God's creation and therefore as worthy of our fullest involvement.

That, however, will require a critical approach to all non-Christian studies or works of art, literature, and science so as to expose their falsehood, to correct them, and to infuse them with a Christian viewpoint. Only that science which honors God will be seen as genuinely producing true knowledge. We may then consider it imperative that we develop a Christian view of astronomy and physics, of geology and biology, of psychology and related disciplines; a humanistic view of psychology will be seen as dangerous and false, but a Christian view of this discipline will claim psychology for Christ.

We may look at other social institutions in the same way. We may see them as evil and unsuited for Christians, but needing to be reshaped by Christian principles rather than rejected wholesale and avoided. We may thus refuse to join non-Christian labor unions, but will form our own Christian labor organizations. We may likewise refuse to work within one of the major political parties, but instead try to form our own political party, or at least our own political think tanks.

The value of this perspective on living responsively in the world is that it deliberately seeks to enhance our responsiveness both to God and to the world in all its many complex dimensions. And it seeks to discover a way to integrate the life of faith with life in the world rather than to compartmentalize them. Yet, this perspective still leaves us having to place severe strictures on our responsiveness to the world that is not, or not yet, Christ like. We separate ourselves from the world without any vision of forming a new whole. We are left in the fallen stance which insists that we alone are right and all the world is wrong.

Is it possible to expose the evils of the world from a Christian perspective without falling into a better-than-thou holiness or the arrogance of the "we're-right-and-you're-wrong" type? Is it possible to celebrate in all its complexity the world's existence, to celebrate all of life, while still confronting forcefully all that is radically wrong with the world?

Confrontive Celebration

A responsive stance that is both celebrative and confrontive is indeed possible. It comes with a confession of faith that acknowledges and praises God as the source of all goodness and grace in creation and in redemption. With that confession, we can take the same stance toward the world that we have taken toward ourselves, namely, a readiness to confess that the best of our works are stained with sin, even as we celebrate all of God's redemptive working in Christ for the salvation of the world. Let's begin with an assessment of how other Christians respond to the world.

Assessing the World-View of Others

In each of the previously noted ways of responding to the world we find something that is positive, legitimate, and even important. We discover something for which we can be grateful, something to celebrate, even if we choose not to follow that way ourselves. I may have no desire to live in an Amish community, but I am grateful for the Amish witness to the priority of spiritual values over material ones. Many of the attempts to make Christian faith relevant have some merit to them as they heighten our awareness of one or another aspect of life by focusing our attention on it. Liberation theology heightens our awareness of the drastic needs of the poor. A psychologized theology of self-esteem does the same for a sense of our own self-worth and that of others. And in the compartmentalizing of religion, even with a humanistic bent, we can value the message that the world deserves to be treated with respect for its own sake and not subjected to the tyranny of a narrow or rigid religious bias. Also, those who seek to stake out a claim for Christ in all academic and social areas of life provide us with an enriching and expansive way of responding to the world. The question is not which way of responding is right in contrast to all the others that are wrong. We do better to ask: What is there in each of these ways of responding that is helpful or insightful? What in each enhances our own capacity to respond to the world in celebration?

Nonetheless, each of these ways of responding to the world needs to be confronted with its own limitations. We can confront all self-imposed constrictions that diminish rather than enhance our responsivity as we live in God's world. We can do that as graciously as possible and as forcefully as necessary because we are aware that our own responsiveness as Christians is also but a small beginning of what is possible for us, and even then is also stained with sin, like the responses of others. Furthermore, each formation of a Christian response to the world has the potential of becoming a form of idolatry or "circumcision," including our own. This occurs to the degree that adherents make their own perspective the measure of all truth and the basis for judging others, or for maintaining unity and fellowship with others.

Affirming the World as Seen Through Faith

Christians are radically changed when they are given the gift of faith. Reconnected with God through faith in Christ, who has restored us to the circle of trust, we are enabled to see both ourselves and the world with wholly new eyes. Faith produces a heightened awareness of sin and brokenness; we now see sin clearly in ourselves and also in the world. Faith also produces a heightened appreciation for the value that God sees in us and in the world he so loved that he gave his only son to achieve reconciliation. We no longer see others, as Paul says, "from a human point of view," for we are "new creatures" who now see the world as already reconciled to God; what determines our relationship to the world is that we have "become the righteousness of God" to the world with a "ministry of reconciliation," as "ambassadors for Christ" (cf. II Cor. 5:16-21). As Christ embraces us with his own righteousness, so we are now called to embrace the world with his gracious way of doing right.

We can see the sin and the brokenness of the world. We can identify it and name it. We can face and explore the many dire consequences of its rigidified responsivity. But we never give sin and judgment the last word. We need not insist that the world, in whatever form we meet it, must conform to us and to our standards to be worthy of our appreciation. We meet the world as it is, and we respond by validating the world as belonging to God. The world does not have to change in order to be reconciled to God and valued by God's people. The world is already reconciled to God and therefore has infinite possibilities for changing and developing in ways that increasingly are responsive to God and to all people. In being a light to the world, we who confess Christ proclaim the worth of the broken world.

Let's consider some of the ways in which we meet the world, and let's explore briefly what it can mean to live responsively in a world already redeemed by God.

<u>In Broken Individuals</u>: We most often meet "the world" in the form of persons whose lives intersect with ours, whether as

neighbors, as fellow workers or colleagues, as clients in our business, as those who share interests or hobbies with us, or as those who participate in civic affairs with us. Or, they may only cross our path momentarily. Often they are not Christians, at least not in the same way that we are. They may be intelligent and educated, successful and apparently happy with their lives, and not interested in God or religious practices. But as we get to know them, we may also discover that they are hurting, much like ourselves. They have wounds that are not very different from our own wounds. They may be going through divorce, or they may have an ill child or a rebellious teenager. They may be angry, deeply depressed, or highly anxious. They may be facing unemployment or a terminal illness. They may be homeless or hungry.

Whoever they are, they are not much different from us. We can see in them the world that is broken, the world that suffers because of our human turning away from God. But through the eyes of faith we can also see in them the world that God has not abandoned but has embraced by his entering into the world's suffering and taking it all upon himself.

Each such person that I meet elicits my own responsiveness. I will experience my own helplessness, but also my capacity to care and to reach out. How these come to expression will identify something of who I am and what road I have traveled on my life's journey. I may be tempted to avoid people with such problems, as my own anxiety rises from being near them. I may be quick to judge and blame them for bringing these problems on themselves. Or I may be inclined to invest my energy in getting them to change so they will become more like me. All of these responses are quite understandable from a human point of view. They are common to all of us. But they are not particularly Christian. They limit our capacity to be responsive in constructive ways.

When I reach the end of all my helpfulness, and experience my own inability to make any real difference, however, I can still affirm the value of the hurting person to whom I am responding. I can treat that person as a person of worth, as someone whom I can trust to be of value to me and to others with me. I can relate to him or her as a person having dignity, however hard it may be to discern. But the eye of faith discerns it, and that is the faith by which we live—a faith rooted in a righteousness that is not our own. In that faith we can stand with those who are hurting and hopeless in the world. We can be with those who are dying. We can confront the evil of the world as we bemoan its suffering. We can find reason for celebration.

In Education and the Humanities: We meet the world in the pursuit of a formal education and in the study of the humanities. We need not withdraw from education because we are suspicious of it, nor do we need to protect education from religious influence by compartmentalizing religion and thus rendering it impotent. We respond more positively to the world when we seek to Christianize the educational process by deliberately bringing Christian principles to bear on every area of study, but doing so can leave us in the position of thinking that we alone have the answers, and then we may begin to feel that we need to condemn every form of public education as ungodly, and all humanistic studies as corrupting.

But Christians can also make a different, twofold response to the educational process. On the one hand, we, along with others, can confront the reality that public education in many ways is not very effective, especially in our larger cities where gangs compete for the allegiance of teenagers, where drugs and alcohol give a more immediate high than does learning, where dropout rates are scandalous, where parental involvement is often minimal, and where financial resources are always inadequate. We can raise questions and highlight issues in our local communities.

But we can do more than criticize. We can maintain the perspective of faith as we view the educational scene. Our faith itself leads us to see the worth of those children and young people who are not receiving an adequate education. And because we know that this world belongs to God and is redeemed by him in Christ, we have the confidence that learning about this world in all its many facets is inherently worthwhile to every young student, whoever he or she is. Hence as Christians we can take a particularly vital interest in the whole educational process of our nation and world, from the pre-school level to that of higher education. Despite, or in the face of, problems still to be resolved, we can celebrate and work for continuing improvement in all educational endeavors.

We will then want our children and all youth to become acquainted with the best of human thought and to be exposed to the best of the fine and performing arts, not just to those produced by Christians, aware that even the best that is produced by Christians will be stained with sin, as will be the best that others in the world create. Neither our best nor the world's best will itself bring salvation to the world. But for that very reason we are free to experience the best that the world produces so as to discover and celebrate what is worthwhile in it. We may participate in it ourselves, and we will want our children to be at home with it. Because we see the best that the world produces to be a response to all that God has made, we can recognize its worth even as we remain aware of its limitations.

Education that is Christian will not be superior just because it endorses Christian principles and practices. Truly Christian education will have the same goal as all education: to enhance the responsive capacity of human beings as they live together in a world redeemed by God.

In Science and Technology: Christian responses to the developing world of science and technology have throughout history all too often been restrictive and condemning. The Copernican revolution in astronomy and Galileo's revision of physics were once heatedly opposed by the church. Darwinian evolution today often meets the same fate. The advent of most technological developments has been opposed by influential Christians, while such innovations have been welcomed by others.

Why have the church and many Christian people so ardently set themselves against the latest theories of science and the latest developments in technology? One reason may be that the church has often equated following the Truth, who is Christ, with the belief that its own accepted views must be regarded as right. If the gospel stands or falls on our being right and the world wrong, then we will need to oppose any new view that calls for revising our thinking. If giving up long-held views on the way heavenly bodies move or the way human beings developed means that we have been wrong, why, then we could be wrong about other things— so the reasoning goes—even about the essential elements of our faith. All of this makes sense only if our "getting it right," our own righteousness, is the central concern of faith.

Once we let go of faith in our own righteousness or our rightness, we are free to develop new responses to the world and to the sciences that study the world. We become free to engage in the study of the world in all its facets. We dare to formulate theories and hypotheses that seem to best account for what we observe in the world today. We can freely debate these theories and disagree with others who advocate differing views. We can do this because the fear of being wrong no longer restricts our capacity or willingness to interact with the world that God has created and redeemed. We are free to enter into the scientific study of all realities in the world of our experience. We are free to celebrate human creativity in the sciences as a gift of God because we no longer deify the results of science any more than we do those of our own theological thinking. At the same time we are free to confront the arrogance of a science that claims to have said the last word on anything, or that insists on restricting our vision of the world as belonging to God and redeemed by him. We are free to question the notion that every advance in technology is "progress." We may even question whether technology, on balance, really advances human life on this planet or will eventually lead to its destruction. In this regard, too, a Christian response to science and the world can appropriately be one of confrontive celebration.

In Business and Industry: Another arena in which we meet "the world" is in the enterprises of business and industry. In this arena, too, we can see the Christian's calling as one of confrontive celebration. We do not need to withdraw as far as feasible from that arena, nor do we need to consider this dimension of the world to be good only insofar as we Christianize our little corner of it. But neither do we need to seal off this domain from the influence and critique of faith.

As we experience the world of business and industry, either as consumers or as entrepreneurs, we can, with the eye of faith, see in it the creative response of human beings to the world that God has created and redeemed. We can celebrate the genius of the small businessman who makes a go of his modest endeavor. We can celebrate the building of a large business enterprise that efficiently brings goods and services to a vast number of people throughout the world. And we can marvel at the creative capacity of industry to produce large quantities of goods that people can use and enjoy to enrich life. We can be grateful for all the employment that such enterprises create, and for the standard of living that is made possible by modern business and industry. We can celebrate all of this and see the hand of God in it without having uncritically to worship business and industry as humankind's ultimate hope.

We can also confront the greed, dishonesty, and callousness that easily afflict any individual businessperson to the detriment of his or her employees and customers—just as it infects all of us as individuals within or outside the church. More than that, we can confront broader systemic issues that arise from the growth of big business and multinational corporations. We can confront exploitation of third world countries, the pollution of the atmosphere and waterways on our planet, and the disregard for the many people and communities affected by corporate decisions that are made on the basis of profit or greed. We can legitimately raise questions about the corporate responsibility, or responsiveness, of business and industry for the total quality of life on our planet—not just in the present, but for future generations as well.

Not mere condemnation, not simple celebration, but confrontive celebration can best guide the Christian's responsiveness in the world of business and industry.

In Politics and Government: As we meet "the world" in politics and government it is not difficult to notice the reality of sin and evil. Throughout the span of history, most governments have been tyrannical and oppressive. The powerful elite have used their positions of rule to enhance their own wealth and expand their territories, subordinating and oppressing the peoples under them. Even in democracies, graft and corruption are often rampant. Special interest groups carry too much influence. Politics can become a cynical game, and those in government are often too far removed from the ordinary people to enact truly just laws. Political and social structures frequently work to enable the rich to become richer while the poor become poorer. Because all of that is true, there will always be a need for confrontation of corruption and indifference in politics and government. Some Christians, understandably, have concluded that government is inherently evil and corrupt and is opposed to the kingdom and working of God.

Nonetheless, the eye of faith can perceive the working of God in the governments of the world. And we can celebrate it! Paul saw it and wrote of it in Romans 13. Politics and government represent the capacity of human beings to rise above their individual impulses and needs by establishing policies and laws that work for the common good. Without this responsive capacity each person would be a law to him- or herself, making oneself the measure of whatever is considered good. Anarchy would prevail. And that tendency, present in humanity as original sin, permeates all of political life just as it does all of religious life in the church. But even as we confront that reality wherever it blatantly shows itself, we can at the same time celebrate the human capacity to be responsive to the needs of the greater society through the working of government. Wherever and to whatever extent that responsivity actually comes to expression, we can celebrate a glimpse of the coming kingdom of God. As Christians participate in the political process and the working of governments, they serve the purposes of that heavenly Kingdom.

In Other Cultures, Races, and Nations: Every nation, race, and culture has an inherent tendency to consider itself special, if not superior, in relation to others. We look at people who are different from us as "outsiders" and "foreigners." They belong to "the world" out there. They may be considered barbarians, pagans, or infidels, or they may simply be looked down upon as inferior or as "quaint." We make our own culture, our race, our national ways, the measure of what is good and what is not. That supposed superiority has been used to justify enslaving other peoples and destroying their cultures. Sometimes it leads to genocide, as in Nazi Germany toward Jews.

Even where national unity has been imposed for decades, old rivalries often burst forth. Tribal frictions continue to surface in newly formed African nations. Ancient animosities have resurfaced among the republics of the former Soviet Union. National unity in Yugoslavia disintegrated into civil war between the Serbs and the republics of Slovenia, Croatia, and Bosnia. Racism in America easily reasserts itself despite the laudable words in the constitution about all men being created equal.

As Christian faith makes us new creatures in Christ, our capacity to be responsive to other cultures, races, and nations is renewed. With the eye of faith we can see the working of God's creative spirit in those cultures that are vastly different from our own. We can learn to appreciate and celebrate the variety of racial customs and cultural traditions and national traits.

Yet, even as we celebrate that variety, we can confront the

evils of injustice and the suppression of human rights wherever
they occur. But we can do so authentically only as we apply the
same standards of justice to ourselves and our cultural, national,
and racial heritage. In this regard, too, confrontive celebration is
appropriate in our relating to "the world."

In Other Religions: Many of us as Christians are quite
uncomfortable when we meet "the world" in the form of other
religions. This is particularly true when we are not merely studying
these religions in books, but are dealing with colleagues or friends
who follow a religion that is different from our own. While living in
Amsterdam in the early '60s my wife and I developed friendships
with several Jewish students and artists. More recently I have
become acquainted with two Hindu colleagues, both of whom are
thoughtful, gentle, and caring persons. A seminary classmate of
mine has become involved with Buddhism. How are we to respond
to those who follow religions other than Christianity?

In the conviction that Christ is the way, the truth, and the
life, we may feel compelled to respond by avoiding those of other
religions as much as possible. Or we may feel it necessary to judge
them as following a false religion and therefore to be lost souls.
Insofar as we do relate to them, we may consider it our primary
duty to change them, to convert them to our own religious faith so
that they will be saved and not spend eternity in hell. Each of these
responses has something to commend it.

Yet, taken together, the above responses limit us. They limit
our capacity to respond in love. These responses all come out of
our fallen situation in which we make ourselves the measure of all
good, and judge others by that. We place ourselves in the position
of having to defend the proposition that we are right and they are
wrong, we have Truth and they follow falsehood, we are good and
they are bad, we are saved and they are lost. On the other hand, if
we deny that this antithesis is reality, we seem to relativize Christian
truth and faith; we seem to imply that one religion is as good as
another and that there is nothing uniquely true in Christianity.

A popular response to this dilemma is to assert that there are
indeed many ways to God, and all of them provide something of
value to us; all of them in the end arrive at the same place and the
same God, even though they give it or him varying names.

Here is a possible Christian response: There are indeed

many human roads to God, and all of them do end at the same place—they all fail. None of them maps out a route by which we can successfully achieve bliss in the divine presence. As a human way to God, Christian faith and practice is as much a failure as is Judaism, Islam, Hinduism, Buddhism, or any other world religion.

Christian faith always starts with confession of sin. That places us on the same level as all other human beings. This faith then embraces God's coming to us with grace, mercy, and peace. *His* coming to *us*, not the way in which *we* come to *him*, is what beings salvation and inspires faith, hope, and love. That is our only hope and comfort for ourselves. That, too, is the hope and comfort that we have for others, including those who have grown up in and practice other religions.

Once again, our faith in Christ as the only Way changes us in how we view those of other religions. We need no longer avoid them. We can no longer stand in judgment on them. We give up having to change them so that they will become like us. We learn to trust them and to respect them as the persons they are, with their limited but real development of religious sensitivities. We become a light that reveals the worth of those who, like us, belong to a fallen world already reconciled to God through Christ.

This Christian perspective enables us to respond by celebrating whatever human insight and beneficial spiritual practices other religions have developed. Yet we are free to confront whatever it is in those religions that is destructive of human life and that limits rather than enhances human responsiveness and growth. We as Christians are particularly qualified to do this because we continually see the same limitations and the same potential in ourselves as we stand in confession before God and celebrate the wonder of his grace. As we relate to those who follow other religions, we live responsively in confrontive celebration of who they are.

In Matters of Social Justice: One of the stark realities with which the world confronts us is the plight of the poor, the hungry, the unemployed, the homeless, and the imprisoned; we live in a world of ethnic, racial, religious, and sexual stereotyping and discrimination, and the attitudes behind these sources of injustice are institutionalized in the politics of nations and in the structures of society. As we face these realities, how can we respond to them out of Christian faith? We can ignore these realities if we choose. We can blame those who have fallen into such circumstances, as if they have simply not worked hard enough or do not have solid enough values to succeed. We can place all the responsibility on them to change their lives. Such responses are common in our world, but they come from the dynamic of the fall, and not from the righteousness of the kingdom of heaven.

In Christian faith we are changed. Our responsivity has been renewed and enhanced by the working of Christ in us. We begin to see the poor and the homeless in a new light. We become the light that illumines their worth, and the worth of caring about and for them. Our concern for justice for them may at times be shortsighted and will often be inadequate; we will be limited by the social mood that dominates the larger society and the political climate of the day. But the spirit of Christ keeps enlarging our responsive capacity. We learn to celebrate the life of the least of God's children in the world. With renewed trust we can confront the injustice still present in a world that has fallen but has already been redeemed by God.

In Environmental Concerns: We meet the world in the entire environment in which we live. We were created to live in a dynamic interaction with all of creation. We were given dominion over all the creatures of God's earth to provide a caring protection and preservation of them so that their life, too, might develop and be enhanced. The garden in which the human pair were placed was theirs both to keep and to till. They were to conserve it, even while they enhanced its productivity.

We have largely lost our responsiveness to earth's environment, and we are only beginning in small ways to recover it. We have allowed automobile emissions and industrial waste to pollute the air we breathe. Many of our waterways can no longer sustain life as they used to, and the fish of the seas contain contaminants which also threaten our own lives as we consume them. The rain forests are being decimated, and birds are losing their habitat and diminishing in numbers. The effects of climate change threaten to melt the polar ice, flooding vast regions.

Through faith we have the courage to confront all the human abuses of earth's environment that we meet. As we are renewed in responsivity through Christ's redemption and reconciliation of the world, we can again celebrate our entire relationship to the earth and its many creatures. No longer can we view the resources and the creatures of the earth as having worth only as they are of use to us in meeting our needs. By the fall into sin we have made our own will and our own need the measure of their good, and we have lost our responsiveness toward them, but as our responsivity is renewed through Christ we begin to see all facets of earth's environment in a new light. We discover earth's immensely varied foliage and all the varieties of animal life as worth preserving and enhancing for their own sakes, not just for ours. We become responsive to the ways in which we can preserve the beauty of the earth for future generations. We develop sensitivity to the kinds of activities that mar earth's splendor and exhaust its resources needlessly. Thus even as we confront our human destruction of earth's environment, we celebrate the vision of a world that is still "charged with the grandeur of God" (Gerard Manley Hopkins, 1844-1889, *God's Grandeur*).

Summary

We have taken a tour of that vast and complex phenomenon which Christians call "the world." We have attempted to explore something of what it may mean for us to live responsively in a fallen world that is nonetheless already redeemed by God. We have noted that Christians, as well as others, will respond to the world out of who they are and what they have experienced in their own life's journey. We have looked at various ways in which Christians have advocated responding to the world, and we have attempted to identify some of the limitations in those responses.

Our objective has been to discover ways of responding to the world that most fully reflect our renewed responsivity in Christ. Even as we confront the reality of sin with its rigidified responsiveness, we want to celebrate the redeeming working of God in all his creation and among all peoples. Christian faith is grounded in confession of our own sin and the celebration of God's marvelous grace. Believing in that grace gives us the new vision to deal with all dimensions of life in this world through what I have called "confrontive celebration."

We have briefly explored what confrontive celebration can mean as we meet the world in the persons of our hurting neighbor, in the realm of education and the study of the humanities, in the pursuit of science and technology, in the enterprises of business and industry, and in the affairs of politics and government. We have also looked at what confrontive celebration can mean as we encounter other cultures, races, and nations that are unfamiliar to us, and other religions that differ from our Christian faith. We have considered in the same light what it means to live responsively as we face matters of social justice and contemporary environmental concerns. All of these deserve lifelong, creative attention as we live responsively in God's redeemed world.

Whatever aspects of God's world we encounter, whether in other persons, in other living beings, or in the world of creation itself, God's gracious rule calls us to a responsiveness that will enhance their being, even as we are enhanced by them. And we will see that it is through such responsiveness, by such "Living Responsively," that God's sovereign name is also magnified!

9 781603 500616